God Knocking on My Head

Linda Kupiec

with Emma Colbourne

Copyright © 2018 Linda Kupiec

All rights reserved. No part of this book may be reproduced,
scanned, distributed, or used in any manner without written
permission of the copyright owner except for the use of brief
quotations in a book review.

First Edition

ISBN: 1726037118
ISBN-13: 978-1726037112

To everyone who gave of themselves and their time to assist me along my recovery — I am forever grateful for your immense love and support.

CONTENTS

CHAPTER ONE

My First Memory

"Where am I?" I wondered, looking around a room I'd never seen before.

I was sitting at a table in front of a few large windows. There were three other tables around me where people were doing some sort of activities. I didn't know what they were doing, and I certainly didn't know what I was supposed to be doing, so I just sat in my chair looking around passively until a lady in front of me handed me a number puzzle and said, "Today, you are going to play Sudoku."

I didn't know who she was, but I listened to her without alarm and accepted her instruction without consideration. There was only one problem: I didn't know how to complete the task. "What is Sudoku? I've never played it before," I replied.

She explained to me, "I taught you yesterday. You played it here yesterday."

I couldn't remember learning how to play Sudoku, let alone ever being in the room before. For some reason though, I wasn't confused, just unaware. I wanted to recall, but I didn't feel anxious that I couldn't.

Shouldn't I know where I was yesterday though? I told myself to remember. When I still wasn't able to, I informed the lady, "I wasn't here yesterday."

She looked at me and said, "Yes, you were. You've been here for two weeks."

I thought to myself, "What? Two weeks? What?" It didn't make sense to me, but I accepted it. It wasn't that I wasn't worried; instead, I didn't know how to be worried, so I trusted her.

I had absolutely no memory for two entire weeks. My life was a tape recorder, but no one pressed the record button – it just played as I experienced the present moment, only the present moment.

I learned how to play Sudoku all over again with the lady who turned out to be my occupational therapist. It was a tiny snippet, but it opened me to the puzzle of my situation. Putting the pieces together began at that moment for me, my initial memory with my 'new' brain.

Ron, my husband, came to visit me later that day. "Okay, at least I recognize him," I reassured myself. He wheeled me into a room looking out onto a city skyline.

I asked, "Where am I? What city am I in?"

He gently replied, "You're at Metro Hospital. We're

looking at Cleveland."

I was slowly becoming aware of myself. "Why?"

He told me, "You were hit by a car while you were walking Kasey [our dog] on May 5th [2009]."

"Oh. Okay." Without actually processing the words to understand their deeply significant meaning, I accepted them with no emotional reaction – a fact is a fact. In hindsight, I believe that was a blessing.

Four and a half weeks after I was life flighted to the hospital, it was finally time to go home.

CHAPTER TWO

Where I Started

Ron searched the Cleveland area for the best neurology rehabilitation doctor to support my unique needs and continue my recovery after leaving Metro Hospital. He chose Dr. Vinod Sahgal.

When he concluded his first assessment, Dr. Sahgal started to talk into a phone to record his thoughts about my abilities. I realized I didn't know the person he was speaking of, but it *was* me. To me, I was the same as I always remembered. But what he was describing didn't sound like me before I was hit at all.

He said that I was bland, but how could I be that way when I used to always talk with excitement and personality? He noted that I needed to work on the fluidity of my talking, walking, and thinking.

We left, and I asked Ron, "What did he say? What

is fluidity?"

He told me, "It is how fast you can do something." Of course he knew. Why didn't I?

I hadn't realized how slow all of these things were and how long it took me. My brain saw me doing it all, so that meant very little was wrong, right? The person he was referring to was not who I used to be. In that moment, I realized I wasn't me anymore. I thought to myself, very seriously, "Will I ever be me again? If not, who will I become? Who am I now?"

It was obvious: it wasn't just about the numerous broken bones or the cuts, scrapes, deep bruises, and nerve damage that I suffered. It was more complicated than that. The most debilitating damage was a traumatic brain injury.

When the car tossed me into the air, I landed on the front part of my head – my mind was suddenly very fragmented. The impact caused the most damage to my left frontal lobe – the area of the brain that manages executive functions such as emotion, logic, language, and planning. The brain injury was considered severe. In fact, Dr. Sahgal told me that I technically had the emotions and reasoning abilities of a four-year-old child.

Imagine the excitement of returning to childhood! For a second time in my life, I believed in Santa Claus and anxiously waited for him to come to my home. Then, imagine the confusion of a child's mind trying to make sense of new ideas. For example, my damaged brain couldn't tell an idiom from truth. My nurse once told me that a little birdie had told her it was my birthday, and all I could think, as I was looking for it down the hallway with open hands, was that I wanted to hold the bird in my hands. I relived both the pleasures and pitfalls of naïve thinking, and I was wide-eyed and ready to discover the world all over again.

My deficits were plentiful – I suddenly couldn't think, do, or process anything nearly as quickly or as well as I could before I was hit. I could walk and I could talk, but I could not walk and talk at the same time because I was too busy thinking and telling my legs how to take a step, even to the point that I would sometimes have to prompt a leg by touching it. I was focusing so hard on walking that it was the only task I could do. It wasn't just physical executions that I struggled with; it was mental functioning too.

For example, when I wanted to use the word 'doorbell' in a sentence, I paused. My brain would first picture a doorbell and then project an imaginary one out in front of me, but even with the visual, I wasn't able to find the word in my brain to get out verbally. Only when I pressed the imaginary doorbell could I begin to stutter my way through the word, "D-d-d-doorbell."

The littlest tasks like these consumed every second of my attention and ounce of my energy. I could not think of two things at once. I was not able to worry or question, to have expectations, or even to judge. For the first time in my adult life, I was living in the moment. In fact, I was so much in the moment that even revealing a face from one's hands, such as in a peek-a-boo game, made me light up with wonder.

I had a long way to heal.

Something new and totally unexpected unfolded to

me during my recovery: the spiritual dimension.

That's what I want to share with you through this book. The best way I can convey the other dimension to you is to present my own eye-opening journey that completely changed my life and my understandings.

Fortunately for me, Dr. Sahgal asked me to keep a journal. I can still remember that conversation.

After the hard tasks that formed his first evaluation of me, Dr. Sahgal said, "You have a job now. You have homework." Excitedly, like a kindergartener, I accepted. I felt important to have a job. He continued, "Write something every day."

The excitement of homework vanished, "What do I write?"

"That's cheating."

I was stunned. It felt like my brain stopped because it was so confused. There was nowhere to go, but he knew I was stuck, so he gave some ideas, "Write about your parents, your husband, and your children."

I thought to myself, "Okay." But then I wondered again, "What do I write about them? Opened ended questions are difficult. Yes or no questions are easier."

I typed nearly every day for years, amassing a lengthy journal. What follows is a condensed version of my writings regarding my amazing spiritual journey. This abridged presentation of my experiences may be a little cut up; after all, as you will read, it was even a puzzle for me at the time. However, it is an authentic and honest depiction of my own growth with God and the other dimension. To help you understand the timing, I have titled each chapter with the date of the first story's journal entry.

CHAPTER THREE

March 8, 2011

It was almost two years since I was hit, and I still hadn't reached my personal goal of being 'me' again, the person I was before I was it. The only problem was that I had no idea where else I could turn to get the support I needed. Thankfully, Ron was still searching for effective options without giving up on my healing. Wanting to find something that worked to benefit me, even if it was unconventional, Ron decided it was probably best to go in an entirely new direction than the traditional therapy (physical, occupational, and speech) I'd been going to since I was hit, or, at the very least, to supplement it. So, after researching and reading up on it, he talked to Dr. Sahgal about starting yoga. They decided that, with the right instructor, yoga would be a wonderful alternative to therapy for supporting my continual healing.

Ron found Polly, a certified instructor, who happened to be one of our acquaintances from church years ago. Together, she and Dr. Sahgal reflected on areas to benefit me along with the patience to support me. They came up with not only some goals, but also the stepping-stones I needed to be able to successfully reach them.

One night, after arranging everything for my first session of yoga with Polly, Ron talked to me about beginning this new mode of healing. I grew confused, "Yoga is a type of exercise, gentle movements in various poses. You just sit and stretch in different ways. It's for the body, not the brain."

He informed me, "I read an article about how good yoga is for making connections in the brain. Traditional therapy works on one particular area at a time, but yoga works with the body and the mind at the same time. Working on using both together, you will be able to make connections that your other therapies haven't been able to help you do yet. Because you will be focusing on integrating your mind and body, yoga can even open up parts of your brain in ways that you haven't been able to since you were hit."

I figured that it was worth a chance because, if Ron was right, I would grow closer to my goal of 'me'. "Okay, I'll give yoga a try."

Two weeks later, March 8, 2011, Polly brought yoga into my life. For many months, I hadn't been able to answer the door because the executive functioning in my brain was too damaged. I was expecting her though, so when the doorbell rang, I walked over and actually opened it.

Polly smiled, "It's wonderful to see you once again."

I invited her in and led her into the family room to talk. Summarizing why she was there, Polly echoed what Ron had told me, "Yoga supports the brain and healing."

Feeling at ease, I thought to myself, "Why didn't I start before? Maybe I couldn't have done it before. It's good I'm starting now. But…if it's so good, why don't more people do it? Why didn't I do it even before I was hit?"

Getting ready to start doing some activity, Polly said to me, "I want to take your lead."

"My lead? I don't know what I'm doing. I can't lead yoga." My thoughts circled in bewilderment.

She reassured me, "You will follow what I do. My intent is to use your abilities to build my instruction. I will let your body and your mind lead what I do."

What a relief. We started, very simply. To some, maybe it would have been a joke, but I followed what she did. While seated, Polly asked me to take my right hand and touch my right knee. I looked at my right hand and lifted it up – I was concentrating hard. Then, I stopped and looked down at my right knee. I was stuck.

I watched Polly model the motion. When she finished, I looked back at my hand, which still waiting in midair for direction. I couldn't just touch my knee. I had to tell my hand what to do and where I wanted it to go in order for it to move. I was concerned, "Why do I have to tell my hand what to do?

I used to just be able to move like this without thinking." I kept focused as I sent instruction to my hand of where I wanted it to go in space. It took several small, choppy movements, but Polly was patient and supportive. Finally, my hand touched my knee, just like Polly's! Success!

After a few successful repetitions, Polly wanted to challenge me further, "Now, I'd like you to crawl."

I didn't want to question her out loud, so I thought to myself, "Crawl? *I'm* supposed to CRAWL?! Babies crawl! How insulting! This is stupid – how is a baby's activity supposed to be *more* difficult?"

Sensing my thoughts, in the gentlest of ways, Polly explained, "This isn't just for you. I use crawling in other yoga sessions too."

"Okay." I had crawled plenty of times before. This was going to be easy.

I visualized how to crawl, got down on all fours, but then I paused. I was stuck, thinking, "Okay, I move my hands and knees, but how?" I could see myself crawling in my head freely, but I wasn't actually able to physically move. With Polly's support, and using my memories as visual references, I completed one crawl. Just one. As I did, I had to tell my body what to do: right hand reach forward, left hand move forward, right knee, and lastly left knee. Each move was individualized, planned, and then executed, tediously and with extreme intention. One simple crawl took all my mind's energy; I had to stay present in the moment because each tiny move needed to be carefully planned and directed. However, because I was determined to do what my brain saw me doing so easily, I focused until I did it.

With one crawl under my belt, I crawled a little more. It wasn't easy; it took so much concentration and thinking. I was still slow, but I got quicker as I kept working at it. Polly encouraged me, "Your brain is relearning connections. Crawling will become automatic again."

As she started describing our next task, I couldn't concentrate any longer. Though I tried to listen to what Polly was saying, I couldn't at all. My eyes filled with tears, "My brain is shutting down."

"Thank you for telling me. Your brain has been doing lots of thinking today. It's time to stop." Polly was so understanding, but I was disappointed in myself that my brain couldn't make it all the way through our first session without feeling overwhelmed and lost. Pausing on her way out, she gave me the silliest homework, "I'd like you to work on crawling for 10 minutes a day."

As stupid as I thought crawling was, I had just realized that I did need to practice. "Okay, I'll try to. I'll see you in a few days." I closed the door behind her, relieved that my mind could have a break.

I sat down on the couch and tried breathing slowly and deeply. I grew calmer and more focused. Polly might have been gone, but I was still thinking about yoga, "If yoga is so good for my brain, why did it shut down? I don't like that it shuts down."

A few days later, Polly returned for our second session. Again, we worked on basic movements. Though easy for others, simple actions were still all I was capable of executing – *my* brain was working harder than it had in some time.

She introduced a new movement, "Raise your right thumb and move it diagonally across your body to your left hip. All the way across the midline of your body."

I knew from studying early childhood education that crossing the midline was important for child development, but, as we persistently worked on the different exercises, I didn't know why *I* was still being asked to do childish things. I was already an adult after all! Although I wondered internally, I chose to keep quiet and just do what Polly instructed.

"Well, that sounds easy enough. I'll just show her quickly and we can move on," I thought to myself as I put my thumb out in front of me. As I tried to mirror Polly's diagonal movement, I struggled.

I still didn't want to let Polly know that I was having a hard time completing the task, so I used inner speech to prod my finger along, "Hmm…this isn't as easy as I thought." I looked at my thumb and asked it, "Why aren't you moving? You need to move. Move down and across."

With intense focus, my thumb started to go where I wanted it, but only until my hand got to the midline. At that point, it just stalled. I was silent. I asked my thumb, "Why aren't you moving any more? Why aren't you finishing the motion?" Despite concentrating hard, I still couldn't move across the midline.

Thinking of a way to get my thumb where it had to go wasn't easy. My hand was stuck. My mind was stuck. *I* was stuck. Eventually, I used my left hand to pull my right one over the midline and finish the motion down to my left hip. *"Finally."*

With practice, my disjointed effort got easier, but I quietly considered, "If this is such a basic skill, why am I still having trouble? Why do I have to relearn how to do it? Are the halves of my brain going to be better at talking to each other now that I succeeded at crossing the midline?" I hoped this was part of getting back to the real me.

CHAPTER FOUR

March 15, 2011

After a few basic sessions of working on crossing the midline and then practicing during the day on my own, I progressed a bit, so Polly started incorporating more into our time together.

"Oh, good," I thought as Polly asked me to tap my head, "I know how to do this!"

We both began tapping our heads, though she was much quicker than my calculated repetitions. Polly questioned, "Is this like being in the rain?"

"That can be fun!" I replied excitedly, wishing I could feel real rain falling on my head. As Polly laughed a little at my response, I felt like I shouldn't have said what I did. I reflected on how others perceived the thought patterns of my new, and still developing, brain as childish. I was a bit disappointed in myself – I used to be so good at conversations before I was hit, but I was suddenly having difficulty knowing what to say.

Pulling me out of my own reflections, Polly proposed, "Let's try something new. Why don't you mimic the expressions on my face?" Nervously, I agreed to attempt the new task. "Let's start with happy." Polly smiled at me.

I wasn't able to understand the abstract feeling of 'happy' in an emotional context, but I had already relearned that smiling was an outward expression that meant 'happy', so I smiled back. Next, Polly made a surprised face. I tried to make one too – I couldn't imitate her this time. I shared, fighting a tear, "I know what it's supposed to look like, but I can't do it. I've been thinking so much this morning; I'm just stuck now."

"Let's move on to something else for today. I'll do some Reiki on you instead. During Reiki, you can lie down while I quietly invite energy in to help you with your recovery. You don't have to think anymore, but you will get to continue healing."

Even though I had never heard of Reiki before and was unsure of what it was exactly, I was relieved that it meant I could rest my mind. I figured I could practice the expressions by myself later anyway; I could see them all inside my memories, so I was pretty sure I could work on them alone.

I chose to give Reiki a try – I certainly had nothing to lose. I lay on the floor as Polly sat down near my head, where she gently placed both of her hands. Lying still with my eyes shut, I could feel my body opening up until it felt like it was wide open. It was taking lots in. I was open to everything, and then my body was giving too.

After we finished, I wasn't at all sure what had happened or what I had felt, so I described it to Polly. Unable to process *what* I felt, she at least found the right word to help me appreciate *how* it felt: reciprocating.

Our session was over for the day, but I had experienced something new. Something I didn't quite understand, but something good.

At dinner that night I shared with Ron what had happened, "Polly did Reiki on me today, but I still don't understand what it is or why it felt different. She said that it is another form of healing, one that uses some sort of unseen energy from the universe. While I lay relaxed on the ground, I felt like my body was wide open taking the energy in. After a bit, I felt myself doing a little giving too. She said that happened because I'm a giver."

"Could she feel the energy too?" Ron asked.

"I don't know, but I'll find out during our next session."

Polly came over every two or three days, but, determined to be able to cross the midline in one smooth, uninterrupted motion, I practiced every day on my own anyway. When I showed Polly my progress, she agreed that it was time to try something harder.

I shared, "When I walk, I have to touch walls and other things as I go along. When I'm just standing still, I rock on my feet, from heel to toe and back again. Dr. Sahgal told me that I do these things because my brain still doesn't always know where my body is in space, and these actions activate my nerves, sending messages to my brain. That way, I am able to continuously cue my brain to be conscious of where my body is. I would like to help my brain get better at knowing where my body is without the constant little reminders. I want to stand and walk naturally again."

Polly considered my challenge and suggested something that might help me achieve my goal, "I think it could be beneficial if we tried to balance on one foot."

Apprehensively, I stood near the railing that separated the family room from the kitchen. I was ready to work on overcoming another setback, but I needed to hold on to something if I was going to try balancing – I certainly didn't want to fall over! Very slowly, I lifted up my left foot until it was just barely hovering over the floor. I put it back down quickly, thinking to myself, "Whew, that was hard!"

Trying several more times with great determination, I was able to stay on one foot a little bit longer. It was an arduous task for me. Even with both hands on the railing, I wobbled, but I always caught myself. Thankfully. I didn't want to look so silly, so I decided I would practice this on my own later too.

When my brain needed a break from the taxing exercises, Polly offered to do Reiki again. I readily accepted; I was interested to figure out what I had felt the last time.

She turned on soft music, and I immediately felt ready to receive, maybe take something. I wondered, "What am I supposed to get?" As Polly asked me to breathe up through the soles of my feet and all the way out the top of my head, I sort of saw a wave, and the top of my head felt like it opened up. Then, I could feel my head move up towards her, reaching, as if it knew what it wanted. I had not consciously moved my head at all, yet there I was, busy stretching it up towards Polly and the healing energy that she was guiding.

After a little while, I felt something come in and out of my head. Unsure how to explain it, yet wanting to share it with Polly, I showed her how it felt in the best way I could. Stretching my arms up and then bringing my hands down to the top of my head, I explained, "Something seemed to come in. Like it was coming from somewhere else and flowing into my head. Then it's as though it left, like this." I raised my arms back up into the air. I repeated the motion with my hands several times, "It doesn't just happen once or twice – it's continuous, but it's not the same energy. It always flows, yet it doesn't recycle."

"I call the top of your head the crown. You're feeling the energy, Linda. The healing is flowing in and out of your crown."

The song ended, but I remained still. I knew that something wasn't finished yet, so I kept my eyes closed to feel the energy. I felt better. I felt settled. It wasn't just a mental feeling; I had a physical sensation too. "I have goose bumps."

"They're not goose bumps; they're God bumps," Polly replied. "You looked like you were more connected than last time. Today was different to me too. While my hands were on your head, I felt a tingling in my left hand, which was over the part of your head that was most injured. That must have been where the most energy was present."

It intrigued me that she felt something in her hands while they were over some areas and not while they were over others because I felt some localized differences too. I didn't feel tingling, but where the doctors told me my head was hurt the most, and thus needed the most healing, I felt intense heat. With such obvious tangible manifestations, I knew Reiki was helping me heal.

What an eye-opening session.

CHAPTER FIVE

March 22, 2011

Although Reiki was growing very important to me, I knew devoting time to exercising my mind and body was key to my continual recovery. Polly took great care in adapting and personalizing yoga to be my brain therapy. Throughout our sessions, she provided me with novel challenges that effectively enabled my brain and body to process and perform in ways I hadn't been able to since being hit.

Pushed to think harder, I was rebuilding connections – I even discovered some that I hadn't yet realized I lost when I suffered my brain injury! I was definitely moving in the right direction. While my recovery was still the main goal, Polly slowly introduced me to basic facets of yoga.

Settling into cross-legged positions on our yoga

mats, which faced each other, Polly suggested we begin the day with an affirmation. Describing an affirmation as a positive, self-loving thought, she asked, "Why don't you choose today's affirmation?"

My mind raced around, but I didn't quite understand; instead, I just sat there unsure of what to say. Interrupting the silence, Polly continued, "Maybe these phrases are too abstract for you right now." Reflecting on my journey with an understanding that I was resolute to keep healing, she shared a word that I could visualize and relate to, "Determined, as in what you are determined to do."

"Yeah. I'm getting better. I want to be the me I was before I was hit," I asserted, knowing that I was determined to get back to the 'me' I remembered. Polly waited for me to expand this feeling into an affirmation. I couldn't come up with anything.

With a soft smile, she offered, "Today's affirmation will be 'I am strong in spirit'."

Wow, those words were powerful. *Strong in spirit.* Immediately, I saw something, some sort of presence. About five feet off to the side from our yoga mats was a black form; it was approximately three feet high, two feet wide at the base, and tapered to a rounded top. A fiery vivid orange emanated out about six inches from all of its sides but the bottom. I didn't question its sudden appearance, I wasn't surprised or shocked by it, and I certainly wasn't fearful of the form's presence. Instead, I watched the flame radiate, simply taking it all in. With openness and curiosity, like that of a child observing something new for the first time, I asked without apprehension, "What is that black form?"

"I don't see anything," Polly began. I wondered how she couldn't see something that was right there. Right there! Even though she didn't, she calmly continued, "I believe and I trust, even though I can't see."

I still wondered what it was. Unfortunately, the form was gone when I turned back from Polly to look at it again.

It had been there though – without a doubt.

After having felt the impact of my affirmation, we repeated some of the movements from previous sessions. Bringing my hand down across my body, I said, "This is getting easier. I can cross the midline without thinking as much as I had to the first time we did it."

"I noticed that too. Your movements are more fluid and you're becoming a little faster every time," Polly acknowledged.

"I think my brain is making more connections." As much as I wished it would be, I added, "It's still not as easy as I remember it was before I was hit though."

"Well, now that you can cross the midline, let's try something a little bit harder." She stood up to show me another exercise; she wanted me to twist my arms around my body from side to side. It looked difficult enough already, but then she emphasized that I should swing both arms at the same time. I had to think so much just to move one, and now I had to move them both...*together*?! She suggested, "Like you are a washing machine."

I did it, but very slowly. As I watched her do it again, I thought to myself, "Why can't I do it like her?

Faster and better." My brain worked hard as I kept trying to improve – I was busy telling my body where to move again and again. The motion got easier over the course of several iterations, allowing me to feel more in control of my progress. After a while, it was too exhausting to keep concentrating on. My brain was ready for a break.

Reiki was such a powerful experience for me that it became the standard way to end my sessions with Polly when my body, both mentally and physically, was feeling overworked. I still couldn't grasp and convey everything about Reiki, nor did I have the mental capacity to judge it. However, it was all so real – things would really happen – so I knew it was important that I devoted time for the deep, relaxed healing energy.

As we began, everything felt more whole than before. I lifted my hands up, connecting the fingers of one hand with those of the other. I explained, "It feels like this, but even more whole."

Polly proposed the best word she could think of to help me describe it, "Integrating?"

"Yes, integrating," I was glad that Polly was able to help find the right vocabulary with me – not for me, but with me. I paused, considering what integrating meant to me and then elaborated, "Integrating…and connecting."

I closed my eyes again, remembering to breathe up through the soles of my feet. I felt, and briefly saw, a gentle wave moving inside my body, just softly flowing throughout me. My head opened up wide. Then, I felt heat as the energy began to heal the damaged areas of my brain. This sensation was becoming routine. While I was enjoying knowing that I was healing, something new happened. Something unexpected. I went somewhere. I didn't physically move, yet somehow I was suddenly someplace that I'd never been or seen before.

The place was reddish, but not a deep red or a solid red. It was a light red with lots of white and a black outline of a large eye. There were long, thin black lines. They weren't straight though; they were squiggly like lightning bolts in the sky, but I knew it wasn't a sky. It was an active place, yet also a calm one. I didn't know what was happening, but something was.

When Polly took her hands off my head, I immediately left this place – I wasn't done yet though. I didn't know what I wasn't done with, but something important had been happening. I asked Polly to place her hands back where they had been. She did, and I went right back to the place to finish.

When I felt done, I explained how I had experienced somewhere new, "But I don't know what I was looking at or where it was."

She asked, "Was it a place of completeness and wholeness?"

"I'm not really sure. I think maybe it was whole."

"I felt the energy come very quickly this time in my hands."

How astounding that we could both feel it. I wanted to know more. "Do other people feel and see during Reiki like I do?"

Polly explained, "Not many people have these experiences and can explain them. You're giving me affirmation. There is good in all of this. It's not good you were hit, but I believe there are gifts as a result, given that your brain trauma already happened. I feel grateful to be here with you."

I shook my head in confusion; after all, she was the one coming to my home several times a week. "No, thank you for coming to help me."

Because my brain was so damaged, I had no choice but to live in the present, be open to everything without fear, and savor every moment without concern. Something bigger seemed to be slowly revealing itself to me through all this energy though. Despite not understanding, I knew there was more. More what? I wasn't sure yet, but nothing about it worried me. All I was sure about was that these little snippets of something, of energy, had to add up to something even more.

CHAPTER SIX

March 25, 2011

While my sessions with Polly were doing different things *for* me by facilitating my healing, such as reconstructing connections within my brain, they were also unveiling new things *to* me. It was difficult to put such abstract and deeply personal experiences into words, but yoga and Reiki both grew more meaningful each time. It seemed that during every session something new would transpire.

As I did yoga, I would feel some sort of manifestation of energy. It wasn't anything that I physically witnessed with my eyes, but rather a quiet and calming unseen presence. Unseen, yet very much detectable. Very much *there*. I could sense its vast, indistinguishable presence. I could feel its abundance. It was so real. I was curious to know more, "Polly, do you sense what's all around us? Can you feel what I do?"

"No, I don't sense in the same way that you do. Although, I can tell on your face when things happen for you."

I knew something was there – maybe it's better said as *here* – to be experienced, but I was a bit surprised to know that my face expressed it. "It's different today. There is more of a fullness, a soft, light fullness all around us. Surrounding us."

As we continued with some very simple yoga, it was as if we were encompassed by something more specific than I'd ever sensed before. I didn't know what the something was, but I was confident that it wasn't bad or evil. It wasn't a person, but it wasn't little either. Instead, it was light and airy, just sort of 'there' around us. It was so new that I silently wondered, "What's the reason? It's just here, but what is it? Is it energy? Or maybe something else?" While I was definitely open to it, I certainly didn't have the answers.

We finished the various movements that exercised my brain and, as had become our norm, began Reiki. Polly was taking her time telling different sections of my body to relax, one at a time. As in prior sessions, she started by focusing on my feet. When she was at the knees, I suddenly sensed something. Some form of healing energy kept trying to enter the soles of my feet, just simply wanting to flow into me. Although I tried to ignore it so I could focus on what Polly was saying, it persisted.

Wanting to be prioritized over Polly, the energy took a stronger course of action. The energy was not fighting me to let it go faster, but to allow it to be fully 'there', in my body. Instead of just trying to flow – I clearly wasn't listening to that – it spoke to me directly and assuredly. It told me, not in a way my ears heard, but more in thought messages, "I'm here. Let's begin this. Let me be 'there'. This (Polly's slow relaxation technique) is stopping me."

I wasn't exactly sure where 'there' was, but now that I had heard the energy's wordless speech rather than just felt its presence, I was compelled to listen. Unsure what to call this particular energy, yet wanting to address it, I gave it the name 'It'. I communicated, without words, but communication nonetheless, "Okay, 'It'. I understand. I'll tell Polly."

I said aloud, "You're going too slow, 'It' is here. You are slowing 'It' down."

Polly, sounding surprised, responded, "Excuse me?"

"You're going too slow. 'It' is here," I repeated matter-of-factly, still unable to question or judge.

"No one's ever told me that before."

As she quieted, 'It' flowed into my body to just 'be there' like 'It' wanted to.

There was intensity while 'It' moved through my entire body, but also smoothness. I sensed 'It' as a wave, a wave without barriers, flowing freely. I knew 'It' was there to heal me, to go coursing throughout my body with healing energy.

When 'It' was ready to be done, 'It' communicated to me, "I'm finished for today."

I could feel the energy's positive impact, "No, not yet. Please continue."

'It' went on a bit longer until deciding, "Okay. Done to stop. Know that I'm always here – I will continue to work with you."

Wonderstruck and with much gratitude, I acknowledged the energy's sense of completeness in a thought message, "Thank you so much for the healing."

Over the weekend, I thought about everything that was transpiring. So much was happening, and it was all unfolding so quickly. It was confusing and difficult to understand, but now that I was aware of the unseen energy's existence, I was beginning to expect its presence. I was no longer just relaying to Polly what I sensed; instead, I was settling into 'being' with everything that presented itself to me. Not just during yoga and Reiki, but all throughout the day too, even during the days Polly did not come. Yes, it was new, but none of it was scary. It was amazing. It was *wow*.

With each passing day, I grew more curious about what was happening. I had recently heard the term 'awakening'. It was a new word for my redeveloping brain, but maybe it could offer an explanation. Unsure, I asked myself, "What exactly is an awakening? Am I in the midst of one myself?"

I wanted answers and was eager to find out if others had similar experiences to mine, but I was sort of scared to tell people about everything. I contemplated to myself, "A few weeks ago, I didn't even know energy existed like this – will anyone else ever understand what's happening now?"

Since I became mindful of the energy for the first time during yoga, I decided to ask my friend Judy, whom I knew did yoga quite frequently, if she sensed any of it. She told me that she never had any experiences. I chose to keep quite because, despite wanting to open up about mine, I wasn't ready to share first.

I did tell my doctor about my experiences. Although he told me nothing was wrong with me in terms of having these new experiences, which was good to know, I still hadn't found anyone who could relate to me or help me understand.

My next session with Polly was remarkable. I was getting comfortable sitting on my yoga mat when Polly said to me, "Should we call the spirits?"

"Call them? Is she crazy? Doesn't she know that energy is always here?" I thought to myself. Then, I continued aloud, blunt and direct, as if it were the most obvious thing in the world, "No, they're already here. All around."

Polly asked the energy, "Please heal and help us."

"Polly, they want to help you. Energy is around you – it's always around all of us. All encompassing. It's here now, and it's calm."

We stood up and started yoga. We began by bringing our hands to our hearts and interlocking our fingers together. As soon as my hands came together, I felt a seal, as if I was coming together with the energy around me.

Polly asked me to raise my hands up. I stretched my

arms upwards and outwards, angled halfway between being straight over my head and reaching out to my sides, with my hands open. As I brought my arms up like this, I felt I was literally in an envelope – safely tucked inside an incredible envelope – I was right in the middle of an immense amount of amazing energy, completely surrounded.

I felt my heart area crack open wide, like a canyon; it might not have really burst wide open physically, but it sure felt exactly like it had. Energy was leaving, but the more I was giving, the more I was receiving back in. Something was right there, reciprocating through this opening. How profound!

I stood taking it all in, reveling in the exchange of energy, basking in an awesome oneness.

All was as it was to be: it is what it is.

Polly interrupted my experience, "Linda, I can tell by your face that something is happening for you. Could you please describe it?"

After searching my vocabulary for a few moments I said, "It's like a communion." That was the closest word I could think of to explain something so difficult to encompass, let alone verbally define.

Polly responded, "The 'something' is love."

"No," I asserted, "It's more. Yes, it's more than love. It's enveloping." I just knew it was so much greater than love. There was so much depth. It was so clear, so amazing. "It reciprocates so much too."

"You've always had an open heart. I even felt that about you years ago when I knew you."

"I never thought of it like that before now." I meant that; I really hadn't. I wondered why I never felt or communicated like this before if I'd always been the same kind of person.

Ready to challenge my brain for the day (remember, this all stemmed from what was just supposed to be brain therapy), Polly encouraged me to retain the position I had just been in and cross one leg over the other.

I did, but I stopped and uncrossed my legs immediately – not because my brain couldn't do it, but because whatever was happening, that energy communion, stopped entirely when I did. It was as if crossing my legs prevented it, like I was blocking the energy. Once I uncrossed them, it all came back.

Polly respected the feedback and asked, "How about you lie on your back and move your legs like you're riding on a bicycle instead?" I watched her demonstrate the new movement, and then I did it too.

The energy communicated with me, "I want to be here with you. You're kicking me away. Stop pushing."

Again I stopped and told Polly, "It doesn't like this."

"What doesn't?" she asked me, interested to hear more.

"The energy! It's like we're pushing the energy away from us. I don't want to push it away. I know that it doesn't want to be pushed away either."

Once again, Polly, respecting my experiences, altered her instruction and found something else to do.

After completing a variety of brain exercises and yoga movements, we concluded the session with Reiki. Polly played some new music. Something wasn't right. I could sense that 'It' wanted to heal me, but didn't. As I wondered what was wrong, 'It' informed me that it couldn't flow with the music that was on. Confused, I asked the energy, "Well, why not?"

"The music is calling me, but I don't want to be called. I'm already here. I'm here and I want to be here," 'It' shared.

I relayed the message to Polly – she changed the music.

As soon as the music changed, I felt heat in my head. It happened so quickly. Polly, whose hands were on my head like always, remarked that she felt a big difference, adding that it happened really fast for her too. The intense energy continued to heal me, feeling stronger and hotter than it ever had before. I even felt a vibration at one point.

I wondered for a moment if I was wrong, if maybe none of this was real. As soon as I thought to ask, the energy responded, "No, you're not wrong. It's real." I knew it was real. It was so evident. It felt so right. I allowed the healing to continue.

The music stopped unexpectedly. The unplanned silence lasted a little while, during which I heard, (again, not with my ears, but 'heard' is the closest way to describe the wordless communication), "Whole and complete." As I internalized the message, the healing energy's flow ceased. 'It' was done. Like right then I was whole and complete. The moment I heard this is exactly when the music, on its own, started to play again. But how could I be whole and complete? I was still so far from the 'me' I was before; my healing was by no means done.

Afterwards, I asked Polly, "Did you turn the music

off and on?"

"No, not at all. I didn't touch it."

I was taken aback. Regardless of the meaning, what a significant and powerful exchange!

When Polly was getting ready to leave, I knew that there was energy following her. I knew that I was supposed to tell her something, but I hesitated because I had never relayed a message from the energy to someone before. Instead, I opened the door and said good-bye. Polly was already at her car when the energy's certainty finally overtook my apprehension. I yelled out, "Energy is still with you; I'm supposed to tell you."

She said, "Of course it is. Everything is energy, even things like wood."

I understood her point, but I had become so aware of the unseen energy during these first few weeks of yoga that what I meant was more, "No, Polly, I'm not talking about when we think. I know we can think of everything *as* energy. But this is different. Everything *is* energy. Energy is *everywhere*."

"So, you just *know* energy?"

My quick answer caught me off guard, "Yes."

CHAPTER SEVEN

March 29, 2011

You must be psychic. That was the conclusion of what she wrote. "Wait, what?!" I asked myself, "What did she write?" Intrigued, I went back to reread the emails.

I had emailed my friend Jackie. *Just want you to know I'm thinking of you and hope all is going well! You were in my dream last night. We were walking on a small sorta wide wooden bridge over water. I kicked something and there happened to be a few bees. But we were okay.* It had felt good to just initiate a conversation, something difficult since my brain injury, even if it was only a written one.

Her reply the following day was entirely unexpected, *It's amazing that you were dreaming of bees because I have an exterminator coming tomorrow. I have a real problem with bees at the San Jose townhome. They swarm all around my patio space. They look like yellow jackets and the exterminator tells me they are paper wasps. They like to nest under the tiles in the roof. The exterminator is going to climb up there and put powder in the crevices to hopefully get rid of them. Maybe his ladder will be white and that symbolizes the bridge in your dream. You must be psychic.*

As I reread it, I thought to myself in awe, "Wow, she really wrote that. She really did." I couldn't believe how my dream and her story were so related. I just kept thinking, "Wow." Jackie's response gave me affirmation and belief for the first time outside of yoga and Reiki – I really was growing more connected to what else was 'there'.

I knew there was energy all around - there was no doubt about that. I felt things, sensed things, and communicated with things. I just still didn't know what it was or what it all meant. I reflected by myself, "How could I have and appreciate these experiences, but not fully understand them? Maybe I should have known more about yoga before I started. I thought it was a way to exercise and balance. It's so much more though – it's a calming experience, and it opens me up to things that never happened to me before. Energies I never even knew existed."

At dinner, I shared these thoughts with Ron. He explained some of the ways that other cultures view energy differently than ours; I was surprised that I suddenly had commonalities with belief systems I had never heard much about before. It got complicated for me to understand, but I felt less alone. As I tried to listen, I thought, "I was just doing yoga to help my brain build connections so I could be the old me again, but it is leading to so much more, a whole new journey…maybe."

The next time I did Reiki, 'It' effortlessly returned, moving throughout my body. For some reason, I decided to put my hands on my crown and my heart, palms turned down towards me. 'It' stopped, communicating to me that it didn't like when I did that. "Hmm," I thought. "Was 'It' not done yet? Did 'It' want to continue? Did I just prevent the healing energy from circulating?" I wasn't quite sure, but I had learned something: it was my choice to be open and allow the energy or to tell it not now.

Polly turned on a track of wave sounds as I moved my arms down along my sides with my palms facing up. I noticed that energy moved in me real fast. Something was certainly powerful about this music, hearing these waves – the energy took me to a place, a place of all white light. I said to Polly, "It's like I'm there. Wherever there is, I'm there."

"Are you at the beach?"

"No, I'm not at the beach," I responded, "There isn't any water. Everything is just a brilliant white." I could hear something – little high-pitched noises, similar to birds chirping. I adjusted my gaze towards the sounds, but I couldn't see what was making them. All I could see was light, lots and lots of white light.

The music ended, and I opened my eyes. Polly considered aloud, "I wonder if you were in your body when that happened."

"That's a weird question…where else would I have been?" I thought to myself.

It wasn't long until I started communicating to energies other than 'It', or rather, until other energies started communicating to me. It all started while I was at home looking for a birthday card in my box of greeting cards and happened to come across a sympathy card for the loss of a mother.

Shortly after seeing it, Ron told me that he just heard our neighbor Lucy lost her mom, Helen. "I just saw the card to send her," I told him, as I continued thinking silently, "Hmm…this seems like more than a coincidence."

Although my brain still couldn't process emotions very well, my memory went into action – I knew that we were supposed to show our support for Lucy by going to the funeral home and paying our respects.

When I arrived at the funeral home with Ron a few days later, I wanted to find Lucy right away. I flew up the few front steps and began searching quickly. Because my injured brain had yet to relearn some of the social norms, Ron had to remind me to slow my behavior. He suggested that we approach the casket before greeting Lucy.

I had never met Helen before, but I felt intensely drawn in upon seeing her body, in a gentle way. I turned to Ron, "I know this sounds sorta weird, but, for some reason, I want to hold her hand."

Obviously he remarked, "You can't do that!"

I knew I couldn't, but something was happening.

There was a connection – one I didn't understand, yet I felt something tugging at me.

Ron broke into my thoughts, "Why don't we go wait our turn to see Lucy now?" I wasn't sure why, but, as we waited in the long receiving line, I found it hard to contain myself.

Eventually, we made our way up to Lucy. I gave her a tight hug. She briefly explained to us how Helen passed, "At first, my mom was really bad, but then she got a little better. She wanted to say goodbye to us without being on any machines, so we had them removed. While I sat and talked with her, I finally told her, 'Now, you're free'."

I softly looked Lucy in the eyes and raised my hands, placing one on each of her cheeks. It was as if cupping her face was an automatic action for me, but it isn't something I would ever do – surely not to Lucy. Unsure of exactly how I knew, words flowed out of my mouth, "She thanks you for that. She was ready to pass on, and those words allowed her to. She no longer worried about leaving you."

As Lucy complimented her mom with many kind remarks, I repeated what Helen was communicating to me, "Lucy, it's you too, remember that. It's what you have done. It's who you are too."

I shook my head, feeling like I needed to get back to myself, "Your mom will always be there for you." We finished our conversation, and I escaped to the bathroom, dumbfounded.

What just happened? So many thoughts were bouncing around in my head. Despite the sadness, I didn't cry when I spoke to Lucy. It was different. I used words and actions I wouldn't myself; I felt like Helen's messenger more than a consoling friend. What did it mean though? How could I even be a messenger?

I was perplexed, never having conversed with an energy that had passed on from this physical dimension before. Reflecting on the conversation I realized, "Something new happened. This is real. It just happened. Maybe I never was before, but I *was* a messenger just now."

CHAPTER EIGHT

April 9, 2011

My new experiences were bringing my old views of the world into question. Trying to make sense of such experiences, I used words and concepts I already understood in an attempt to describe them. I knew there was something special, maybe even spiritual, about my wordless conversations. While reasoning with myself for a reference point, I compared them to prayer.

Before I was hit, I prayed often talking to God. However, I was no longer limited to prayer as I used to know it; oh no, there was certainly more. Despite this new communication reminding me of prayer, it was by no means familiar – not just because my brain was relearning things after suffering a traumatic injury, but because the messages took on such a new form. I didn't have to use words to convey myself, and I wasn't limited to talking with just one entity; energy was in and around everything. So much more than I ever thought before – I simply only needed to be open.

There was even more than thought messages; when I allowed it, I could *feel* the energy. I reflected how during these moments my body would sort of smile – what a good feeling. It was gentle, and even though I wasn't sure why, it seemed there was not a worry. I felt absolutely free and just knew *oneness*. As I asked myself, "A oneness to what though?" the word completeness came to me. It was weird because I wasn't so sure of what that word meant. My brain went through a lot during its trauma and recovery, and now words were suddenly coming back. They had context now. Even though I couldn't define words like completeness, I knew them. More importantly, I felt them.

I grew concerned that since so much new was happening, I might never be able to reach my goal of getting back to the old me. Yes, my sessions with Polly were helping my brain, but they weren't just the peaceful, therapeutic exercise I thought they'd be. They were opening me to something bigger.

I grappled with who I was and who I might become, "Is there a new me now? It's a new journey I seem to be on, so does that mean I'm a different person? Does a different path mean I give up on healing to who I was before? I won't give up healing – I want to be me – the old me. I liked that me. So, should I stop yoga? Would not doing yoga or Reiki anymore help me focus on getting back to the 'me' I miss, instead of this new stuff, like all the energy?

Everything started when I began yoga and Reiki, so if I stop, then won't all these new things stop too?"

I wasn't sure I was ready for them, so I considered, quite heavily, quitting. Then I realized, "It's not scary at all. Yes, it is confusing because I am experiencing things I never have before, yet it's all calming. I have seen and heard new things, powerful things even, but nothing has been bad."

After deliberating with myself, I decided, "I don't want to stop."

I was forming a fuller picture of both the world around me and myself. I shared my new thoughts and views with Ron and then listened as he reminded me about what he had shared before regarding how different cultures view energy. Still a bit too abstract for me to fully comprehend, I was again amazed as I listened to him talk about how other people already felt and believed in what I was just now being exposed to for the very first time.

Not only was I beginning to unite my own thoughts with my new experiences, but I could also tell that my brain was healing and rebuilding its connections as my personalized yoga required less and less concentration and effort. I could actually see myself progressing. Smiling gleefully to myself, I knew I was getting better!

Determined to keep improving, I looked forward to my next session. When the doorbell rang, my dog Kasey excitedly ran to welcome Polly, anticipating the treat he had grown accustomed to getting from her. After she acknowledged him, she turned to greet me,

"How are you this morning?"

"I'm okay, but one of my children suffered a concussion last night," I shared.

Her response was unexpected, "Why don't we dedicate some healing energy during Reiki today?"

Even though I was uncertain whether or not anything would happen, I knew I wanted to help in any way I could, "I'm willing to try."

We went ahead and did some yoga first. Then, when we began Reiki, I allowed the energy to enter my body. Like always, I felt the wave sensation flow throughout me, but this time I asked it to redirect itself. A few moments later, I declared to Polly, "That's real." Over and over I just kept feeling like I knew it was real. I knew the healing energy was going to help where I guided it, where it was needed. I wanted Polly to know how real it was too, "Wow, it really works. I'm certain of that."

Polly smiled and then turned on a different song so that I could have time for 'It' to heal me as well. When the music ended, I felt like I actually woke up. I didn't feel like I was ever sleeping though. Curious, I asked Polly, "Did I fall asleep?"

"No, not at all."

"Hmm. That was different. It really felt like maybe I had." I wondered, "If I hadn't been sleeping, then what happened? Where was I instead?"

Lucy volunteered to drive me to an appointment for speech and occupational therapy one day when my friend Neysa, who usually drove me, had a conflicting appointment. Yes, traditional therapy was still a small part of my recovery. I was sitting quietly in the car with Lucy remembering what had happened at the funeral home. I wondered how to start a conversation about it without her thinking I was odd. Although I was nervous, I asked her, "What do you think about energy, like the unseen energy that is all around us? Do you believe in it?"

"Yes, and sometimes I feel like I have a sense of it, like from a distance I can feel things. When I see a bird fly, it's as though I can feel the air under its wings." Encouraging me to share what I had been experiencing, she mentioned our last interaction, "After everyone had gone from the funeral home, I told my sister, 'I don't remember much about the day, but I do remember some things that Linda told me.' What you said really stuck with me."

I thought to myself, "Oh gosh, wow, she remembers what I said? Not much else, but what I said? Me, of all people, *ME?!*" I knew at the time something wonderful had happened at the funeral home, but I was astonished that it had an effect on Lucy too. A memorable one at that. I was glad I could be open with her. I said, "It wasn't really me. Your mom was there."

As our conversation flowed, I began saying things, things I didn't even know, things personal to Lucy that only her mom would have known. I wasn't thinking about what to say; yet, these words were flying out of my mouth. Lucy listened very intently, nodding along to acknowledge their significance and truth.

I was befuddled. "What is going on?" I thought to

myself. Then, I listened to my words more carefully. As I was telling Lucy these things her mom knew, I was saying 'I'. I was talking in first person about personal things between Lucy and her mom. Huh?

It hit me: I wasn't relaying messages anymore; I *was* Lucy's mom. Helen was using my body. She was talking through my mouth as herself.

Woah. I wasn't ready to let others use my body as their own to speak from. Relaying messages was okay, but not someone taking control of me. I shook my head to get Helen out. I communicated with her, not wanting to close her off entirely, "Please stop. Please don't use my body to talk directly to Lucy. I will tell her what you want me to say."

Helen respected my request and, instead of speaking with Lucy, communicated with me. Now that I was talking as myself and passing along Helen's words, I said to Lucy, "It's me again – it's Linda talking again." As Helen was still talking to me, Lucy expanded on the thoughts her mom had just shared. I had to ask Lucy to stop talking so I could better listen to her mom – I couldn't have two conversations, one with Helen and one with Lucy, at the same time.

Just as at the funeral home, the important message that Helen wanted me to make sure Lucy knew was how meaningful it was to have heard Lucy say, "You're free."

It was such a persistent message. I told Lucy, "I'm not sure why this is so important, but it is. She wants you to understand that she is glad you told her she was free. She really wants you to know how important it was for her to hear those words because she had been worried about you. I don't know the meaning, but she wants you to know."

Shedding a few tears, Lucy whispered, "I know why."

When Lucy dropped me off at home she got out of the car to say goodbye with a hug. I realized it hadn't been me hugging her back, "That hug was from your mom." Just as I did before, I shook my head to get back to being me and said, "Now here is a hug from me." Hmm…it felt different as I hugged her from me.

Lucy said one last thing before getting back into her car to leave, "It is a gift that you have been given."

That night, I shared my day with Ron over a steak dinner. I knew he was becoming more open to the unseen energy that I was experiencing; however, he didn't welcome it like I did, so I just gave him a quick summary of what happened with Lucy and Helen.

When I finished sharing, he proposed, half joking, "Why don't we give the fat on the bone to Kasey?"

"Your dad would have done that with his dog." Right when I said 'your dad', it was as though Ron's dad, Al, who had passed away a couple of years earlier, was right there – in energy form, of course. "Ron, do you sense your dad's presence?"

"No."

Despite how suddenly it had come, it was so strong – like *WOW*. I pondered quietly, "How doesn't Ron know? It's his own dad." While wondering how he could be so oblivious, I started to receive a message.

"Your dad wants you to know he is in a good place." Ron was rather quiet, so I continued, "He says that he wasn't as strong as people thought he was. Is that true?"

Ron didn't have a verbal reply, but he nodded his head in acknowledgment.

Al kept communicating to me. He also wanted Ron to know that he was proud of him. He said he'd never told Ron. Surprised by that, I wanted to know if what I was hearing was even true, so I asked Ron aloud, "Did he ever tell you that he was proud of you?"

"No," Ron answered curtly. After a few silent moments, he elaborated, "I knew he felt that way though."

Yes, I had heard Al correctly. I could tell Ron was uncomfortable though, so I told myself that it was time to stop. Al had something more he wanted to say to Ron; I thanked him instead, expressing that since Ron wasn't ready, I couldn't say anything more.

Before falling asleep that night, I reflected alone on my day. How truly affirming it had all been! I was connecting, disconnecting, and changing the manner of communication between my physical dimension and the energy one. The things I said were coming from somewhere else, someone else; they were things I didn't know, things I myself couldn't even understand. But they weren't just words to others. They were meaningful messages, so deeply understood by their intended recipient.

My mind drifted to the last thing Lucy had said to me, "A gift? What is the gift exactly? More importantly, what do I do with it?"

CHAPTER NINE

April 21, 2011

Polly told me that she had to cancel one of our upcoming sessions, as she would be going out of town for a few days. I was extremely disappointed – yoga and Reiki weren't just important for my brain recovery, they were important to me, personally. I didn't want to miss out on anything meaningful! Knowing how I felt, Polly arranged for her friend Krysti to do Reiki with me in her place.

When Krysti came over a few days later, I was nervous. I had never done Reiki with anybody besides Polly; I wasn't sure if this was going to feel as positive. Luckily, all my concerns vanished when, as soon as we began, I felt the energy's presence just like I had during my other Reiki sessions.

Then, something different happened – good

different, of course. I felt that I was part of the energy in the room. I was connected to what I had previously only sensed enveloping me. Energy swirled around me, and this time I swirled with it. We were interconnected, the energy and me. For the first time, I knew with certainty that my energy was somewhere else.

My energy didn't have to stay contained within me; it could be somewhere *outside* of my physical body. How incredible!

After about twenty minutes of Reiki, Krysti sat down on the couch to chat. She was the first person I met who had first-hand experiences similar to mine and was open to sharing them. I anxiously pulled my chair close to her, excited that I had someone who could relate to me.

When Krysti began to share, I tried to listen intently, but something distracted me. My attention was being pulled elsewhere. I shifted my gaze towards the floor. Something was there. I saw a few small, thin, light colored lines like airy, translucent ribbons softly moving within the small space between us. I watched as faint reds, yellows, and oranges streamed together.

It hit me: I wasn't just sensing energy this time – I was actually *seeing* it. Energy was flowing out from each of us to travel together. I watched as the energies combined to form some sort of figure eight. Caught up as they swirled around our feet, I was no longer paying attention to Krysti.

She realized something was going on, "I notice your eyes are moving. What are you seeing?"

I looked up at her, "My energy and your energy are traveling together. They are meeting near the floor, intertwining. I can actually see them, with my own eyes." Hoping she was witnessing the beautiful, colorful flow too, I looked back down to watch it more, maybe understand it better, but everything was gone.

Krysti had not seen anything, but she assured me that she had no doubts about anything I experienced.

When she left, I realized there might be even more that I didn't know than I had thought. I was still learning so much, and I was thankful to have spent time with Krysti. I didn't feel as alone.

When Polly came back, she brought something new with her to yoga: some stones. Except, when she showed me the book she also brought with her to accompany them, I learned they weren't called stones. The title said something about healing with crystals. Hmm…that was hard to understand. What an abstract concept. To me, they were just a few stones, but she started to explain to me how they each have their own properties. Well, that was something I could identify with. I was suddenly eager to understand more.

Polly first presented the largest crystal she brought – a long and thin piece, about ten inches long with a one inch squared base, slightly jagged at one end. It was a translucent, lustrous white. She said, "This is selenite."

Just looking at it, I felt it had a strong presence – so much energy to it, even emanating from it. Without thinking, I told her, "Wow, that's powerful."

She asked, "Do you want to hold it?"

Pulling my hands back, I told her, "I don't know. It's like I can't. It's too powerful for me. I can sense its strong energy. I'm not worthy enough to touch it and be around its presence."

"Of course you are!"

With her urging, I held it. I felt an immediate connection to it, as if it had belonged in my hands all along. "There's something special about this, Polly."

"How about you hold it while we do Reiki today?"

When we started, I laid the selenite on my chest. I could feel the energy, but something wasn't quite right. A bit unexpectedly, the selenite communicated to me in its own wordless speech. It was showing me how it wanted me to hold it. Following its advice, I picked up the piece of selenite and held it so that the jagged end was pointing upwards and outwards. After I did, I felt stronger energy invited in. I felt more whole, even more connected to the universe's energy, just by simply changing the mineral's orientation.

Relaxed, I was appreciating the healing taking place until I felt something hefty on my neck. "Wow, Polly, something is happening on my throat. It feels strong. I'm not sure exactly, but it's a heavy feeling. Not painful heavy. Maybe weighty would be a better word."

"A piece of stone, a tiny little sliver, broke off the crystal and fell onto your throat."

"Gosh, it is powerful!"

When the song finished, I felt ready to end Reiki. Before I got up, Polly picked up the piece of selenite that had fallen on me. Assuming it was going to be a large piece, I was astounded when she showed it to me. It was only a centimeter long, about the thickness of a piece of thread. I was surprised Polly had even been able to find it after it fell! I wondered, "How could it have felt so heavy, so weighty, so substantial, when it's such a little, tiny piece?!"

Polly handed me the piece before she left. As soon as she'd gone, I found a little piece of blue ribbon and taped the selenite to it – I was definitely keeping that special sliver.

While in the car with Ron the following week, I noticed thin clouds high above us. They weren't stretching straight along the horizon, and they weren't a flat blanket above us. Instead, they looked very light and wispy, energized by a gentle flow as they slowly shifted in the air high, high above us. Curling together, they formed almost a swirl across the sky.

I observed the clouds with fascination – taken as a whole the image reminded me of my own energy during Reiki, swirling in and out with other energies. Even though I couldn't see the energy during Reiki, I thought the clouds looked like how it felt, or rather how I sensed it. It was spectacular. I asked, "What makes the clouds look like that?"

Ron informed me, "Cold and warm air meeting as clouds traveling different directions get close."

Mesmerized, I stared up at the sky to watch the clouds and their movements. I thought, "Wow. Air must be powerful when it meets. What an abundance of energy coming together, just like during Reiki. But where does the energy come from?" I still didn't have the answer.

I quietly dug deeper into my own thoughts, "So, what is the energy? Who talks, well really communicates, with me? Are they the energy?" Trying to create some sort of framework in my mind, I decided, "I know that when I'm open, there is more communing. I still don't know with whom, but I know it's good. There's energy all around. There's bliss out there."

When we got home, I searched online for a quote I had heard, "I must be willing to give up what I am in order to become what I will be." I learned it was from Albert Einstein. I read the words a few more times. What he said resonated with me deeply, very deeply. I reflected on why it was so relevant to where I was in my life, "Am I supposed to become someone else? But...I just want to be me again. I don't want to become someone new. Why was I hit? Was it part of God's plan? Why me? Who am I now?"

I spent the following few days anticipating my next session with Polly. I was looking forward to holding the amazing selenite again and feeling the energy's intensity. When she arrived I excitedly asked, "Where's the selenite? I'd like to hold it again."

"I'm sorry, Linda, but I forgot to bring it with me."

Disappointed, I went to get the blue ribbon with the little sliver on it. After we completed yoga and I was situated for Reiki, Polly placed the miniscule thread-sized piece on my chest, where I had previously held the larger one. She put her hands on my head to begin Reiki. Even though it wasn't the entire piece of selenite I first had, it was still really powerful. The energy from the selenite didn't care about the size. How remarkable!

The energy came in, swirling quickly; it was as though even more than 'It' was communicating with me. The energy was so powerful at times that I had to turn my hands over, to face my palms down, just to slow it.

I was just about to ask Polly if she could feel all the heat that I was sensing when she said, "I feel so much energy. At first, it was on both sides of your head, but now it is mostly on the left, where you had the most damage."

"Wow, so you can feel it too when it's really strong." Although we had talked about it several times before, I was still glad to hear some affirmation.

As we continued, I could feel a great deal of energy swirling in my lower body – not in my legs, but around my navel area. It was strong and fast. My body wanted to lift up from the floor. I was thinking, "If I look down, could I see myself off the ground?"

We finished and I told Polly how it felt.

She asked, "Was it a feeling of floating or more like lifting?"

"As I felt lots of energy in my lower body, I thought I lifted just a bit and then hovered right over the floor."

"Your hip was very injured. Do you think the energy was busy healing it?"

I considered this, "I think it was more than that. I have noticed that when I'm more open, amazing things happen. Maybe I'm very open today."

We talked a bit longer, and Polly shared something about herself with me, "My mom passed away when I was just 5 years old."

Without giving my response any thought, I replied hastily with something I had never known before, "You have one brother and no sisters."

I somehow just knew it.

"Yes, Linda, that's right."

We were silent for a few moments. I realized that her mom was communicating with me, and that's how I knew. Then I said, "You are wholesome." Hmm…wholesome certainly wasn't a word I used. "What does that mean to you?"

Polly had a tear, "I know what it means."

CHAPTER TEN

May 19, 2011

My aunt, my mom's sister, was dropping by for a visit. I was looking forward to spending time with Aunt Katie – I didn't get to see her often. Before she arrived, my mind was spinning as I tried to come up with a solution to my internal debate: I wasn't sure if she, or anyone else (besides Krysti and my little, but very important, recovery team of Ron, Dr. Sahgal, and Polly) for that matter, would truly understand me, "Should I share my experiences with people? If other people aren't always ready to hear what I have to share, am I supposed to say anything to anyone at all? I don't even understand everything…how might someone else? Should I tell Aunt Katie? I think she believes in unseen energy and Reiki. She's a nun with great compassion for people, but, because she's also an attorney, she can also be blunt in telling it like it is. It's risky to confide in someone who loves me but might not understand and shut me down instead."

The afternoon was warm, but when she arrived, her presence made it warmer yet. As we sat outside conversing, I remembered the comfort and ease I always felt talking with her, even as a child. I decided to tell her some of what I'd been experiencing. She listened with interest, and, to my relief, echoed some of my new beliefs, "When you were in the hospital, Sister Sheila came to do Reiki with you a few times."

"I always liked Sister Sheila. I only remember her coming to the hospital once, and even that is a very vague recollection, but maybe she helped me start healing. Energy is everywhere, and the energy during Reiki is really powerful. It wants to heal and help us. What do you think about energy?"

"I think it is all around us, too, Linda. Everywhere, so much so that it is even in black holes. It really is all around."

I shared some of the conflict I felt between my old and new beliefs, "All of this is making me question who or what God is; there is so much more than I had thought before. Who or what do you think God is?"

Her reply was straightforward, "It's vast. It's bigger."

Wow. She understood. She believed. She knew too.

I reflected on my new perspective more deeply after she left. Through talking with Ron and Aunt Katie, I was beginning to understand that many religions had the idea of energy right. Still, it was more than any of them could convey. I thought, "It's not so important what a religion calls it – it just is, and, wow, how vast it is to so many others too. A fullness of energy reaching everywhere, one that I never felt in this way before. Maybe more people than I thought really do understand. Maybe the words we have in our vocabularies just aren't able to express the vastness of energy, limiting us from talking about it."

After dinner, Ron showed me a TV program about people who had suffered traumatic brain injuries. Each of them was sharing their own recovery – some of them could do remarkable things after being injured. For example, one was suddenly able to play the piano! Watching it got me thinking, "I can't do anything new with my hands, but maybe that is like me in some way. This is new, what my brain does. How I just know and communicate with energy. It's not what I do with my body. I'm not sure exactly how things happen, but I know that what happens is real. I don't want it to stop."

Ever since the impactful 'strong in spirit' affirmation two months ago, I had been saying it at the start of every session I had with Polly. I was ready for a new one. I knew that my journey, my spiritual journey, was one I wanted to continue, so I said to Polly, "I'm ready for a new affirmation."

Knowing that my brain still had a long way to go in my recovery and the affirmation had been too abstract for me last time, Polly offered, "Okay, would you like help coming up with one?"

"No, I already have something in mind: openness

to my journey."

"That's a wonderful intention for today!"

Ready to begin the session, I confidently repeated, "I am open to my journey."

Later that session, during Reiki, I found that the energy didn't feel as powerful as it had before, even while I was holding the selenite crystal. I realized that I was thinking about what to have for a snack instead of being in the moment with 'It'. I told myself to stop worrying about my snack and shift back into the present moment, that doing so would help.

Shifting did give me a way to free my mind and better connect. I wasn't able to stay in the space with 'It' for as long, but I was glad I hadn't closed down all the way. I thought, "When I said my affirmation, had I already known that other things were flooding into my mind and preventing me from being in the moment?"

After being hit, my brain was so damaged that I had no choice but to live in the moment; now that my brain was getting better, I was starting to have to actually *try* to be in the moment. I had to put effort into focusing and not letting other thoughts in. For the first time, I had to consciously remind myself to be open to 'It' and all the other unseen energy.

Not wanting my experiences with the energy to stop, and having gained more confidence interacting with the energy, I tried new and different ways of being with the other dimension on my own over the next few days. I found that I didn't have to be restricted to Reiki or yoga for 'It' to heal me; I just had to allow the energy. 'It' was always with me when I wanted to be with 'It' – ready to flow as soon as I invited 'It'. I learned that when I was more open and more settled, when I was calm and relaxed, I could connect better. The more willing I was, the more willing the energy was, and the stronger it felt.

CHAPTER ELEVEN

June 4, 2011

"You're not alone," Polly had reminded me. "Even though I don't have the same experiences as you, I don't want you to forget that there are people who do. What you experience is real. It's important that you remember you are not alone. Maybe you'd benefit from talking and sharing with people who have similar experiences." She offered me some information about a seminar.

I was hesitant, but I took the pamphlet anyway. While discussing it with Ron that evening, he offered to drive me so that I could attend. Nothing seemed to be stopping me; instead, pieces felt like they were falling into place. With no excuse not to, I decided to take a chance and sign up – I hoped that it would help explain the things happening to me a little more concretely, or at least some of them.

When I arrived, it was strange. Not strange weird, but strange new. There was a stack of cards on a table near the door, from which we were all asked to pick one. I had never seen cards like them before, but I followed along and chose one anyway. My hand just went to one – I didn't take a long time to make a decision about which one to take, something that was a bit unusual for my healing brain. It was as though I already knew which one I was supposed to choose before I was even asked to.

Still unsure what it was, I watched as everyone else turned theirs over, so I flipped mine over too. On the backside, it read, *"You are at the end of a cycle in your life. Call upon your angels to comfort you and to guide you to your next step. Happiness awaits you now."* Woah, that really resonated with me because of everything that happened since getting struck by the car. My life changed, and I was finding that I was moving in a new direction.

The words stayed with me as I introduced myself and explained my brain injury and the spiritual journey that had recently begun revealing itself alongside my healing journey. After all the participants gave their brief backgrounds, the facilitator for the day asked that we each find a partner to give messages to. She wanted to give us an opportunity to practice communicating with the other dimension in a safe and welcoming space.

I paired with the lady who had been seated next to me. When we sat down to begin, she handed me a necklace. I was confused, but I took it from her anyway, thinking, "Well…What am I supposed to do with this?"

Immediately, I felt a connection to someone from the other dimension. I just knew something – this wasn't always my partner's necklace, it had first belonged to her late grandmother. I realized right then why my partner had handed it to me: she wanted to connect with her grandmother. Effortlessly, I started to share messages from her grandmother.

When I finished relaying some thoughts, my partner shared her astonishment at how accurate everything I said was, "I've been practicing communicating with the other dimension for a while now. I still struggle being able to read for someone else. I can't believe how much you just received from my grandmother."

She might have been impressed, but I got a tear. The session leader came over, "Are you okay?"

"I just did something I had no idea I could do," I said, slowly, in awe of even myself.

My partner verified, "It was so amazing - she was right on with everything that she was telling me."

I said, "I was only repeating what I was hearing. Well, it wasn't a voice. But there was communication. Wordless speech, more in thought, and I just verbalized it the best I could."

The seminar leader explained, "A medium is someone who communicates with another being who is out of their body. That's what you just did. You have a special gift for it. You are a medium."

"Out of their body, that must mean like an energy, one from the other dimension. It's what I've done before, but I didn't know it was called anything special," I was thankful to be learning the vocabulary and glad to finally apply the right words to meanings I already understood from my personal experiences. I certainly didn't expect anyone to be impressed, let alone tell me that I had a gift. To me, everything was so obviously communicated.

I paused for a moment in disbelief, reflecting inward, "Wow. People think I'm a *medium*."

We all switched partners for a second round of messages. This time, my partner was trying to read me. I tried to be open for it to happen, but began talking to her instead. Without realizing what I was doing and saying, she said to me, "Wait, you're doing a reading on me. I am supposed to be doing a reading on you right now."

"Well, all I'm doing is telling you what I'm hearing. I'm sorry."

She explained to me, "You are good at this, but you can also say thank you to the person in spirit and stop. You don't have to keep relaying the messages."

"I appreciate you sharing that. I might be good at it, but I don't have the language or all the understandings of it yet."

When we got back into the whole group one of the ladies I did a reading on said, "Linda was communicating with my spirit guide during the messages."

Uh-oh. That made me nervous! I asked the group, "The terminology is all so new to me, is that good or bad?"

Everyone clapped for me until someone answered what I was so eager to find out, "Yes, it's good. It actually takes many people quite a bit of training and lots of time practicing to be able to do."

Another participant added, "It is so natural for you. It is like you were born to be a medium."

"I wasn't born this way, but maybe it is a result of my traumatic brain injury."

I recounted my conversation between Helen and Lucy, even how Helen used my own body to interact with Lucy. The others were surprised; some commented that allowing something like that to happen was difficult and uncommon.

"Still," I told them, "It was weird that I had to refocus just to talk as myself. That I had to shake my head and tell Lucy, 'Okay, it is Linda talking again.'"

The seminar facilitator said to me, "You're in control. You can tell the spirits that you will communicate only by repeating what they want you to say, that they can't use your body to communicate directly. That's okay to say."

We paired off again to do a final reading. This time, to allow it to be more involved than quick messages, we went outdoors and found a quiet place to sit with our partner.

I began channeling, relaying messages from the other dimension. Something was different about this connection. For the first time, I noticed something more than wordless messages; I also sensed my partner's mom's loving energy gently surrounding her like a soft cloud.

As I communicated, I felt strength and importance behind the messages. I didn't know why I was saying some of words I was or what they meant. In fact, some words weren't even part of sentences and certainly didn't seem like they belonged in a reading at all! (For example, I felt that randomly saying the word 'ankle' was quite out of place.) It felt so real that I relayed everything anyway – I knew to keep going.

When we were done, my partner told me, "My mom passed away two years ago, and the words you said hold so much meaning to me."

I was curious if they truly did. Testing myself, I asked, "Did the word 'ankle' mean anything to you?"

"Yes, I sprained my ankle three times. In fact, everything you said resonated with me. Everything was true."

I walked away from the seminar with deeper understandings and higher confidence in myself. I thought, "It was nice to be with like-minded people and discover more about myself. It's not necessarily easy to learn I have gifts, but I am thankful for the terminology and positive feedback. Am I truly a *medium* now?

"That's not easy to learn. That wasn't part of who I was before I was hit, and my goal has always been to heal back to that person. Should I set a different goal...?"

On the way home, I shared with Ron what happened during the seminar and concluded, "I feel more open."

He responded, "You were always a gentle person and really nice, so it would be easy for people, energy, or spirits, whatever is trying, to communicate with you."

I had previously noticed that I connected with

some of the seminar participants more easily than others. His reply prompted me to wonder if everyone has different energy and whether or not I connect stronger to those who have similar energy as mine.

CHAPTER TWELVE

June 6, 2011

I was still healing, so Polly was still coming. During Reiki she played a song that I really liked the time before. It was gentle. The last time I heard it, 'It' felt like waves inside me; this time, I felt like the waves myself. The high notes in the song felt like angels all around me, very close, as if enveloping me and saying, "Take it all in."

Then, I had a thought conversation with energy, not the energy of anyone in particular who had passed away, just enveloping universal energy. More importantly, I wasn't asked to relay the messages to anyone. They were all just for me.

I was told, "Develop what you've been given."

"But what have I been given?" I asked.

"Take time. It takes time, be patient."

"But...I don't understand."

"Allow it to unfold. Take steps to develop it. Trust me. I'm taking good care of you."

I wondered about what I was supposed to do next, how I was supposed to develop this, and who was taking care of me.

Opening up to the healing, I asked Polly, "Can you feel the heat on my head? The left side, the front section?" The right side didn't feel the heat, but, then again, it didn't need the strong healing since it wasn't as severely damaged as the left.

Knowing about my damage, she answered with another question, "Do you notice that you tilt your head to that side during Reiki? Can you feel that it moves to the left?"

"Yes, I notice it. I don't intentionally do it though. It's as though I'm subconsciously reaching for you, your help, the healing energy that you're inviting for me."

I asked again, "Polly, can you feel all the energy? Its intensity?" Even though she had confirmed it during previous sessions, it was new enough that I still looked for reassurance. I wanted her to remind me that I wasn't making anything up, that we could both feel what was happening.

"Yes, I can feel it."

How good to hear that! As the energy's strength grew, I became overwhelmed. The energy was so, so busy. I became so hot that I wanted to rip my blanket off, which never happened before. I got a tear and communicated to 'It', "I want to stop."

'It' replied, "It's not time to stop yet. Stay calm. I

will take your energy to a calming place of whiteness so that your body can continue to receive the healing."

Suddenly, I was in this calming place. Well, my energy was. 'It' had been right – the healing energy continued to flow throughout my body, my brain in particular, without overpowering me.

When 'It' was finished, Polly described something different she had felt, "When I had one hand on each side of your head, I felt the energy go back and forth. It was moving between my left and right hands, like the energy was making connections between the different halves of your brain." Yes, I knew I was healing, but to hear Polly say that she really felt the heat going back and forth, that she actually felt connections being made, that she felt *healing*, was a true testament to the energy's extraordinary effects.

I overheard someone talking about the chaos of life and thought, "My life isn't chaos. Some days might be, but not my life now. Maybe it can be a little confusing because my experiences are still new, but my life has clarity. In fact, it has never been clearer than now, since my experiences with the other dimension started. It's more like: what is, just 'is'."

I wanted a way to share these insights of my own with others, but how could I? Sure, I knew about the other dimension, but I was realizing that some of it was more unknown than known. What's more, I didn't know how I could share something that was still partially unknown to me with others.

I remembered talking to Ron about the clouds and

how their abundance of energy reminded me of Reiki. It was only a small reminder though. Similar, but not nearly as incredulous. The unseen energy was so much more – how could I possibly represent such a vastness?

A week later, I was still searching for a way to illustrate the other dimension. I went outside to try to draw some of the things I experienced. I didn't get very far, but when I returned back inside, I felt a good difference: my brain felt freer. I wondered how this simple task could help my brain. Then I realized that because drawing was so hard for me, I hadn't thought about a single other thing while I was outside. When I first started healing, I couldn't think beyond the task at hand. Now that my mind was healing, it was able to wander…and wander it did! This challenge of drawing the other dimension allowed me a way to stay focused on the present moment. I hadn't tried to stay present; in fact, I didn't even know I had until I went inside. I had simply allowed. What a remarkable change it made!

I considered the difference between the terms 'allow' and 'try'. Allowing was more about being in the moment, but trying was thinking during it. I reminded myself that when I allowed, I had experiences and felt a complete oneness. I decided that I needed to find ways to remind myself to allow and be open to 'all that is'.

I was waiting to tell my friend Ann Marie about my new spiritual journey in person, but it was growing so much that I couldn't wait any longer. I hadn't been able to see her for a while though, so I decided to share with her on the phone. As I was summarizing a little bit of my experiences, I could sense her grandmother was right there with me.

I described to Ann Marie her grandparents' house and the apron her grandmother wore while working in the kitchen. I went on about how, in that moment, I just knew how much her grandmother loved baking and cooking. Ann Marie listened intently. As I took a step back, I detailed the door leading out back and the beautiful flowering tree near it. I stopped myself to clarify, "Wait, maybe it was more like a bush."

Ann Marie spoke up with confirmation, "Yes, there was a lilac bush."

I wasn't even *with* my friend, just on the phone. It was still a bit strange learning so much through the other dimension concerning someone I wasn't even physically sitting with. Wow, another new experience! Though it was quick, I learned that it was something more I was able to do!

Wanting to get my old personality back and just be 'me' again, I focused heavily on healing my brain. However, there were so many physical injuries that still needed attention too. Polly started a session with a broad question to address them, "Why don't you ask your body what it needs?"

Surprised, I wondered how something like that takes place. I wasn't sure how I could ask my body something like that and hear its answer, so I asked Polly, "I can try, but how?"

She had me stand, just simply stand, with my eyes closed, "This is going to be a quiet activity. Let's start with your feet. Concentrate on how they feel, how you sense them. Do you notice any differences between them? For example, are they different colors? Don't answer out loud, just notice how they feel today."

She gave me silence to connect with myself. Nothing special happened. Hmm, I wondered if I was doing it right. Afraid to question her, I asked only myself, "How is this going to help? Nothing is happening."

Next, Polly asked me to notice my ankles; again, nothing.

Just as I was beginning to think we were wasting time, Polly asked me to notice my legs. Suddenly, I noticed a difference between them and thought, "Oh my gosh – Polly was on to something! This has to be what she meant! There is a difference! My right leg is heavy and grounded. My left leg is like pieces, not leg pieces, but like fireworks or twinkling lights."

Unexpectedly, I fought back tears. My left leg was pretty damaged when the car hit me. I knew that. I still felt the nerve damage every day, almost constantly. Now, I was truly sensing the damage in a whole new way, but I wasn't supposed to talk out loud, so I held it all in.

Polly asked me to move up to my stomach area, to take time to notice it. I couldn't fight the tears any longer, "I need more time. I'm still focused on my legs because it's like I don't have my left leg."

She stopped the exercise, "What's wrong with your left leg?"

"It doesn't know – it's extremely confused."

"Why don't we do Reiki now so you can focus on

healing?"

I smiled, "That's a good idea."

Once I was ready to invite the energy in, Polly prompted, "What is the happiest part of your body? Focus on that."

"My heart. Well, not my physical heart. I really mean a spot in that same area, but the heart where I can connect with the energy and commune. The one that felt like a canyon opening when I communed." I paused, thinking about how to refer to it, "My energy heart. When I open my energy heart, things are calm, a complete oneness. I like my energy heart. My energy heart is the happiest."

"Now, take a few moments to notice it." After a minute or two, Polly continued, "What area of your body needs the most healing?"

I assumed it was going to be my left leg since I had just sensed it was extremely confused, but I took time to feel the energy to make sure. Instead of where I thought the energy was going to focus on, I realized there was heat in the left, front part of my brain. "Well," I thought, "I guess that needs the most healing right now."

Letting the energy go where it was most needed, I began to sense a figure eight of energy leading from my energy heart to my brain.

After the first song ended, Polly played another one and suggested, "Why don't you ask your left leg what it needs?"

I did, and, to my surprise, I got an answer right away. It was obvious, "Connections." The nerves were so damaged that my leg just wanted, and needed, connections.

I had goosebumps as the healing energy flowed to my leg. When it was finishing for the day, angels and healers were right there holding me, gently wrapping me up within amazing energy.

I shared with Polly "The angels communicate differently. When they talk, I sense their voices as high-pitched noises, more like sounds – like how dolphins speak. It's real, but it's different because it's harder to differentiate sounds to words."

"Do the angels guide the healing?"

"Oh, I don't know. All I know right now is that they are radiant, radiant forms."

A few days later, Ron and I were in the car and a song came on. It had some words in it about angels flying. I turned to him, "Angels don't fly – they're just there. They're just here. They want to help, and I know they want to be thanked. Sometimes it might be hard to be open and allow them to, but they really do want to help."

"Why do they have wings if they don't fly?" Ron asked, referencing all of the depictions of angels that surround our human lives.

I was confident, "They really don't fly. They're pure energy."

CHAPTER THIRTEEN

July 19, 2011

About two months after sharing my new experiences with Aunt Katie, she came back over to visit with me again. As we spoke, I looked for her brother, Joe, who passed away a year prior. I hadn't expected him during our last visit; however, since I had gained confidence communicating with the other dimension, I assumed that he would have messages for us this time. Unfortunately, as much as I waited for him to be present, he didn't show up.

Eventually, I put him out of my mind and enjoyed the conversation with Aunt Katie. It was only when she was getting ready to leave that I sensed Uncle Joe's presence. Interrupting Aunt Katie, he was calling for me to listen. I knew it wasn't polite, but I kept breaking eye contact with Aunt Katie and looking to the side.

Even though I couldn't actually see him with my physical eyes, concentrating on the space where his communication came from helped me focus on what he wanted to share. He informed me that he was worried about his wife.

When I heard that, I stopped listening and looked at Aunt Katie in concern, "When will you be going to visit Aunt Rita next? I would like to see her."

"She is frail, but we can go on Tuesday, just for the afternoon."

"Yes, please, I'd love to." As I said my goodbyes to Aunt Katie, I felt a little worry grow for Aunt Rita.

Tuesday arrived, and Aunt Katie and I were on our way. When we walked into the familiar house, Aunt Rita was lying on the couch, curled up under a blanket, with her eyes closed. With a big smile, I said, "Hi, Aunt Rita."

She opened her eyes and looked up at me, "Linda, it's you!"

As we enjoyed a light lunch, we reminisced about the mini-vacations I spent there as a child. By the time we finished eating, Aunt Rita had grown quite tired. We took it as our cue to leave. With a bit of sadness, I hugged and kissed her good-bye.

It had only been about a week since Aunt Katie had taken me to see Aunt Rita, and I was already back, this time with Ron, visiting for her funeral. How glad I was to have gotten to see her one last time!

Ron and I took our seats for the service, and, right away, I began to sense so much. There was so much love present. I knew there were angels in the church. When the service ended, we walked across the street to the cemetery where a man was waiting to symbolically release a dove. As he let it fly, I looked up, feeling my energy swirl upwards with all the beautiful, positive energy celebrating Aunt Rita's life. It was incredible how much there was to just feel and be a part of. Everyone started to walk over to the luncheon, but my gaze was still fixed towards the sky.

Breaking off my flow with the energy, Ron asked, "Who are you talking to or listening to?"

My energy stopped swirling above in order to respond, "No one specific, just lots of energy. Lots of presence. Why?"

"I could tell you were interacting with energies. Your body got so much more relaxed and your face looked calmer, like you were not worrying about anything at all."

I didn't tell him, but what he said was all true. The energy, the other dimension, it all felt so peaceful. I felt such gratitude to be with it. There was a unique calmness – I didn't have to worry at all. I was more relaxed. Who wouldn't be while they were part of this blissful energy?

Ron and I went over to the luncheon to greet my cousins and spend some time catching up. Once again, Uncle Joe was communicating with me. He was asking me, more like strongly nudging me, to go apologize to one of his sons on his behalf. I had no idea what it was about, but, listening to Uncle Joe's insistence, I followed his directions and made a beeline to my cousin Dave and said, "I didn't know anything happened between you and your dad."

He looked at me as a gaping expression came

across his face, "What? I don't think anything. What?" He was clearly confused.

I paused a moment. It was wrong of me to start off with such an accusation. I didn't pass my uncle's message on. Instead, I had interpreted it myself and asked my cousin about it.

Realizing I couldn't turn back now, I shared, "It's kind of new, but I can communicate with people who have already passed over to the other dimension. Your dad wants me to tell you something." I carried on with the true message, the one intended for my cousin, rather than my interpretation (which hadn't made as much sense), "Your dad wants you to love yourself, and he says that he loves you. He says it's more than love or being proud of you, it's a special connection. He loves you, and he wants you to do what makes you happy."

Dave opened up to me, verifying why his dad's message was so important and deep to him.

Uncle Joe kept insisting that I say one last thing, but it was time to go. I shook my head and communicated, "No, we are done."

He communicated with me, "But you *need* to tell him that I didn't know I hurt his feelings so much, that I'm very sorry I hurt him."

I was ready to leave though. My brain was still healing and the day had already been long enough. I was done. I didn't pass on the last message.

On the way home, Uncle Joe scolded me, "I wanted you to tell him that, and you didn't. You didn't tell Dave what I needed him to hear. It was important." He was very disappointed in me. He kept repeating himself, persistent that his son needed to hear his apology. When I got home, I sent a sympathy card to Dave, complete with Uncle Joe's message.

It had felt like such an exhausting and draining week already – I knew that being with the other dimension was calming and healing, so I retreated to the quiet of my room, settled on my bed, and opened my energy heart. I liked the feeling of my energy swirling high above. It was so special.

I felt the oneness, thinking to myself, "Yes, the energy is me. It's not the physical me. My energy leaves my body, but it's still me. It's the spiritual me."

I asked 'It' to heal me. Like always with 'It', I felt the energy flow into my body so effortlessly. It was calmer, not as intense as before. I decided to ask 'It' what was different, "Why isn't it as intense as before?"

To my amazement 'It' communicated back to me, "Most of the healing has been done."

What an incredible moment, and how elated I was to hear that I was almost healed! At the same time, I was slightly worried about losing my new abilities. I thought back to when everything began. My crown opened, my energy heart opened, and I became a part of the energy around me. If I healed, would I stop feeling the closeness and oneness? After all, I didn't have these experiences before my brain injury.

Now that I could feel, really *feel*, I didn't want it to stop.

Instead, I wanted to focus on the things that everyone kept referring to as my gifts. *Gifts.* "Now," I instructed myself, "It's time that I develop these gifts."

A few days later, I closed my eyes and allowed the energy. I saw a closed door, a solid white door. It beckoned me forward, beckoned me in. Not with words, just with the beautiful, brilliant light that scattered out around it. I was just standing there, looking, unable to take my eyes away from the spectacular light. When I finally looked down, I saw light brown footprints leading from where I stood up to the door. I didn't move though. I wasn't running away, but I didn't enter either. My feet just didn't move.

I knew that behind the door was a peaceful place, one where I belonged. It was a good place, powerful in a sense, but not in the human definition. Unsure of who 'They' were, whether they were energies, angels, or something else entirely, they wanted me to walk in. 'They' wanted me to follow this new path, my spiritual path, telling me that I didn't have to show anything to anyone to prove I healed back to exactly who I had been before. 'They' knew that was the goal that consumed me. 'They' wanted me to let go of such earthly demands and walk through the door, telling me that one day I would, that it was meant to be.

I took it all in, but something prevented me from going any closer during our entire interaction. I wasn't ready to get any closer, but I did wonder, "Who is behind the door? Is it energy? Is it the 'oneness'?"

I was suddenly refueled to pursue my new path. Despite having already earned a Bachelor of Science and a Master's of Business Administration, when I was in my forties I felt called to become a teacher, so I went back to school and earned my Master of Education degree and Teaching Certificate. Now, my path was winding another new direction, and I was being called to develop the gifts I was given during my recovery. But where could I turn to help me this time?

Looking for answers, I went to a spiritual church service for the first time. I was raised Lutheran and continued to practice my faith throughout my adulthood. But, with my new framework still under construction, I wasn't sure how all my beliefs would come together.

I considered religion and church a little hesitantly, weighing my old beliefs against my new self, "I'm beginning to question my religion – should I feel guilty? I know what energy is now from my experiences, so my beliefs have changed. Well, they haven't changed, they've expanded. It's not that I don't believe, but that I believe in more. I believe more broadly. Before, my belief was finite, limiting, as if it could be put into a box. Now, because I know, my beliefs are greater; in fact, they aren't 'beliefs' anymore, they're just 'knowns' to the new me." I reflected on the term God, or at least the one I knew growing up. It didn't feel like an encompassing and inclusive enough term anymore, so I decided, "God is more; there is so much more that I think calling God 'The All' instead is more fitting."

I knew it was good to connect with like-minded people, so I listened closely to everyone at the spiritual church.

That day, a man shared, "We must first call on people who have passed in order to communicate with them."

Well, that was a bit deflating. It didn't resonate with me at all. My experiences began before I even realized what was happening. I didn't try to connect. I didn't ask for anyone to be present. I was just so open that I allowed energy to connect with me. I never had to call on anyone to communicate with – they would show up when they had a message. In fact, when I waited for Uncle Joe, he hesitated. Only when I stopped looking for him did I receive messages.

I turned to someone, "This is all still new to me. A car hit me while I was walking my dog, and I suffered a severe brain injury. During my healing, I started to experience the other dimension. All of this amazing energy. People who had previously passed away would appear and ask me to convey messages to loved ones. I wasn't searching for any of it, but it is suddenly so easy. I don't know how I do some of it, but I do. It all just happens."

The response I received left me in awe, "You are very fortunate – you received natural abilities. Some people want to be able to do everything you're describing and spend years practicing and developing such gifts."

I told her, "I heard that we should all meditate thirty to forty minutes a day. I haven't – I don't even know what meditation is! I feel that when I just open up, it happens anyway. Everything is always calm and peaceful. It's really just a wow."

She said, "You don't have to meditate. Just listen to

yourself. You don't need to try and seek, you're already connected."

I felt like I was finally gaining a foundation for my spiritual awakening, but apparently it already bloomed within me. My job was to find ways to nurture it.

CHAPTER FOURTEEN

September 21, 2011

Despite sharing with some of my closest friends, I was still reluctant about being public with what was happening to me – I felt like it was too much of a taboo topic. To my astonishment, the more I opened up, the more I found people supporting me.

For a few days, something inexplicable had been nagging me to visit my dad's best friend Lee and his wife Nancy. I didn't typically think about them so many times in the course of a few days, but suddenly something was quietly encouraging me to go. Unfortunately, due to my brain trauma, it was difficult for me to pick up the phone and make calls, so I didn't. I couldn't believe it when, within a couple of days, Lee called. No way could that have been a coincidence! Right away I asked, "Are you going to be home for a visit this afternoon? I've just started driving on my own again and would love to stop by."

"Of course! We'd love to see you too!"

As always, Nancy greeted me warmly when I arrived, "We're so pleased you're here! It's so good to see you acting like you again."

From the inside, I didn't feel like I was back to me at all; however, I had been hearing this quite often. I didn't understand why, but people were telling me that I was beginning to have a glow about me, that my personality was finally glinting through. I didn't go over with the intention to, but I was feeling so good about my recovery that I began to share my experiences.

I confided in Nancy about my communication with energy and those who had already passed away. Unsure what sort of reaction I'd get, I asked, "Do you believe in things like this happening?"

I was pleasantly surprised with her response, "Yes, I do. More importantly, I believe in your experiences because I know you. I've known you for so long. For you to say it's happening, I know it's real."

I asked, seemingly out of the blue, "How is Dave?" Dave, Lee and Nancy's son, had lost his wife, Patty, years before. It was that moment when I realized why I was there, visiting with Lee and Nancy in their home: Patty wanted me there. She started communicating with me, and, all of a sudden, I was sharing her personal messages.

Lee and Nancy were so open that they actually wanted me to keep going. They wanted to hear what Patty had to say.

Near the end I relayed, "She thinks of you as much

more than in-laws, more like parents."

Nancy got a few tears, "Yes. She told us that frequently." I knew that the credit was not all mine, but Nancy supported me with validation, "Linda, you just showed us how real all of this is. How remarkable."

That night, I considered the significance of what had happened, "I do all these new things now; there is no question whether or not it's all real because the messages are so personal and resonate so strongly with their intended recipients. I know it's all real, even if I'm still trying to fully understand it."

Deep in thought, I considered how I got to where I was, "Why do people sometimes ask if I'm angry that I was hit by a car? I tell them that I don't resent it. It's as if, 'it is what it is'. I trust. But why do people ask? Why are they being negative? While healing, why think of it and build anger? It's more important to focus on getting better, on healing, the positive. Negativity isn't good. So, if I don't resent being hit…why is my goal stuck on being just like the 'me' I was before I was hit? Change can be good; maybe I can even go beyond the 'me' I was.

"Yes. There's more to become. I like the gifts I've been given. I didn't ask for them or seek them out, I couldn't do these things before, but why not embrace it all, hold my hands out, take it all in, and embrace it?" I paused, "Sure, embracing sounds like a good idea, but…there's just a big BUT."

Polly came over for yoga and Reiki, but we spent a considerable amount of the session talking instead. I was happy to share everything that was happening out loud. Expressing my experiences gave me the chance to think about what I was saying and feeling, and, besides, Polly was always interested in hearing about them.

I explained to Polly the door I had seen, the one that I couldn't see with my physical eyes but had presented itself so vividly. "I've seen it a couple of times now, so it must be meaningful. It is calming, as the other dimension always is. Everything is safe, nothing about it is scary, and yet I avoid it. Each time, I see the light beckoning me, but I never move. It doesn't represent death. That I am sure of. I'm gently nudged, not pushed, to go through it by an energy outside with me – I'm not sure who. I haven't moved closer yet, and still I know I will walk in eventually. It's odd because I don't know how I know, but I do know that I will. Just not yet. Why don't I accept their invitation?"

"Is it because you're not ready yet?" Polly asked.

"I don't know what ready looks like to me. I don't know what is 'ready'. Maybe the door is part of my new journey. Maybe it's about accepting that new part of me. Maybe the reality of the earthly dimension prevents me."

Trying to encourage me, "What's the worst thing that could happen if you walk through? The best thing? The range of possibilities?"

I thought for a moment, "They're all good." I silently worried, "But. It's just that…it's a change for me."

"Would it be a big step?"

"A special step, a different step. Not to say it's big,

but it's unique, complete, and wonderful. That I know. So why don't I go?" I wasn't prepared to answer that question yet, and I wondered if I ever would be.

She suggested, "Why don't you go inside your body and find out where or why you're not ready to continue on your spiritual journey?"

I could feel it deep within myself. As my crown opened, the exchange was apprehensive; I was holding back on something that I had done so easily before. I explained, "I'm a little stuck. There's like a little ball that's tucked inside. There's a small part of me that still wants to just continue being who I was before. I want to prove to myself and everyone else that I'm healed, that I'm me again, and these gifts weren't a part of that me."

"Since we can't do anything to change it all right now, would you like to do Reiki?"

I tried not to think about the conflict between an old me and a new me, but it was hard. Then, the universe's energy communicated to me, "You know better now, it's important only to you, your *human you*, that you prove your healing. It's only important in the earthly dimension. You know now that there is more."

My spirit self did know what I should be doing, and the energy was kindly reminding me. The only problem was that my healing brain was capable of questioning once again, questioning which dimension I belonged in and how to be happy in both. I worried, "Am I letting down this new found dimension by beginning to resist? Why am I resisting? I like the other dimension, but I don't want to let go of this one. It's just hard to trust." Yes, I trusted in everything that had already unfolded;

however, I was scared to trust such a drastic change in my own direction, away from what I thought I would do in my life. I was tentative to embrace the other dimension while I enjoyed the earthly one.

As I thought that, the energy shared, "You can be in both, don't worry. Trust."

A couple of weeks later, I was *still* grappling with the dilemma of how to balance my spiritual journey with my healing journey, thinking, "Why is life so confusing when I now know more than I ever have before? Like, from these experiences, I know so much. Why is it hard to trust when I know to trust? When I know it's real?"

I knew that 'The All' had a plan for me, that divinity had a plan, but I wasn't ready to let go of proving my healing. I knew people changed over time, but, at the end of the day, I wanted to be the old me again. I liked that me. I was happy as that person. That was my goal from the beginning, and I wanted to prove I could reach it. I was in conflict.

I knew conflict was not good, and that divinity was good, actually, beyond good. As I considered this, I saw a small group of various human-like energies, a sort of personal panel, from the other dimension. It wasn't tangible, but it was as if the other dimension was projecting it for me to witness. I don't think I saw it with my two physical eyes, but it was there in front of me, right at the crease between the wall and the ceiling. It was a small image, but I saw an oval table with a fuzzy outline of four or five heads sitting behind it. I didn't know these people, and I couldn't make out any details of them. They didn't speak, yet somehow I knew they were there to encourage me to let go and move along on my spiritual path. They wanted me to embrace it.

I wasn't ready. I negotiated, "I will, but not yet. First, I would like to show I'm healed. Then, I will do what I'm led to do on this new journey."

There was a pause, but they understood that it was so important to me. They understood that I needed to take my own little detour.

A few days had passed, but I was still wondering if I made the right decision negotiating with my panel. I asked Ron, "What am I supposed to do?"

"I don't know."

I was beginning to shift from just witnessing and communicating with the other dimension to accepting that I had a spiritual journey to take. My framework was certainly growing and filling in. I just wasn't ready to embrace it all yet. I sighed, "It's hard to make sense of this all. I don't even know what all the gifts I've been given are."

As I said that, I received a response, not from Ron, but from the other dimension, "It's not important, just trust. Smile and trust – it is all amazing."

We went to our Lutheran church that weekend and during the sermon our pastor asked, "Where do you go to be free?"

I knew my answer. I didn't even have to think. I told myself, "To the other dimension. I feel complete freedom in the other dimension."

CHAPTER FIFTEEN

December 8, 2011

As my brain continued healing, I was growing more and more aware of the differences between who I was before I was hit and who I was becoming since being hit. I knew I wasn't the 'me' I wanted to be. I didn't have the emotional connections that I used to have, even to Ron and my own children. I cognitively knew who they were, but I didn't *feel* – I wanted that part back. I also knew that my personality was still somewhat missing. I wasn't able to react or respond the same, interact as 'fun', or converse as fluidly. I heard the same general reaction over and over, which was put best by someone as, "I really liked the old Linda, but the new Linda is okay."

Even though I had been working hard on my healing journey for two and a half years, I was starting to understand that I might never heal all the way back to the old me, that this new me could be as close to her as I'd get.

Disappointed in myself and looking for some sort of direction, I asked Dr. Sahgal, "Am I a new person?"

He paused for a moment, "Of course not physically, but in some ways yes because your brain is relearning everything. It has to mature again, and it can't do that exactly the same way as it did the first time."

That made me sad – I liked the person I was before. I silently panicked, "What if others never like the new me? Wait...what if *I* don't even like the new me?!"

I shared more about my spiritual journey and some of my newest experiences with him. I also shared some of the hesitations that were preventing me from diving headfirst into this new journey, "I know I should be allowing more. I know from the other dimension that I should be pursuing my spiritual journey, but sometimes I turn my back."

He instructed me, "Believe in yourself."

Bam! Right there, in that powerful moment, my brain instantly freed up. Amazingly, hearing those three words made everything just come together.

Leaving that day, my brain was calmer. I didn't feel as lost.

I reflected on his words again later that night, "I am a new me. Yes, sometimes I am hard on myself for it, but everything I went through is a lot – it doesn't matter what other people think or say.

"I am gentler on myself when I allow myself to be

present with the energy. I am centered. I love that feeling. I feel more myself at that time, or during that time. All is such a calm oneness. It's inexpressible, yet real, with much inner beauty and knowledge. Why would I want to go back to a me that didn't have this knowing, that didn't know my spirit self, when it's how I feel most complete?"

A few weeks later, I went to Dr. Druzina, my primary care provider of about twenty years, for my annual wellness visit. When she walked into the room, her face lit up with happiness for me, "Wow, Linda, look at you! You're so fortunate! I can't believe how well you look compared to the last time I saw you!"

"Well, I've been focused on getting better. I'm very lucky that I have been healing, even if it has been a slower process than I would like. Well, some of the physical healing, like my broken bones, was relatively quick. The time it is taking my nerves and my brain to heal is a whole different story though…but I'm still determined."

"I think since you started out at a high level and have been so motivated, your brain has been better able to heal. If you were someone who, for example, sat and watched TV all day, your brain would have had less of a chance to build connections."

I was proud of how far I'd come. In the beginning, I did watch a lot of TV, but I watched certain game shows too, ones that I knew helped my brain. I'd put words together and answer questions. Sometimes, I'd even watch educational programs. I'm glad people could see the hard work I put in.

I explained to Dr. Druzina, "I use my old brain to teach my new brain. I use the memories that I have from before I was hit to figure out how to do something all over again. It's like I have a built-in roadmap for my brain this time around. For example, Ron does almost all of the cooking right now, but one night I volunteered to make the mashed potatoes for dinner. When he asked if I was sure, I reminded him that I had made them many times in my life, so of course I knew how. As dinner was approaching, he told me that it was time to start making the potatoes. Getting up to start, I froze. I pictured a beautiful china bowl full of mashed potatoes baking in the oven. I knew they had to be hot. I first wondered if I had to mash the potatoes up and then put them in the oven. I shook my head, telling myself that wasn't right. Then, I thought I had to bake the potatoes in the oven first and then mash them, so I needed to start with normal baked potatoes. But then I shook my head no. I knew that my mashed potatoes never had skin on them, so that wasn't right.

"I kept visualizing the finished product, but I still couldn't figure out how to turn the potatoes into it. Finally, my memory kicked in: I had to cut the potatoes and boil them! I needed to start with hot water, peel the potatoes, boil them, and *then* mash them. My old memory actually acted like the guide for my new brain figuring something out for the 'first' time.

"Sometimes, before I start something, I wonder if it is new to my new brain, whether or not it is the first time I'm doing that particular activity after being hit, and then when I realize how hard it is to do, I know it's the first time. It's kind of bizarre to have a new brain in a way."

She was interested, "Maybe you are supposed to be doing something new. I believe that everything happens for a reason. Do you?"

"I know that it does. I know that now more than ever before."

"Maybe you're supposed to help people suffering with brain injuries"

I opened up to her and shared my new spiritual experiences. She told me, "I believe that happens. You're the third person I've met with special gifts like that. You have a real mind-body connection."

Another person just referred to what I could do as gifts. Wow! It was really starting to sink in. I told her, "I think that this new path is the one I'm supposed to be following. I don't want the gifts to go away. I think I have so much to share from following my spiritual journey. Even though I feel clarity about that, it can be very confusing at the same time."

She understood and supported me, "I believe in you. What do you have to lose?"

It was something to have my friends and family believe in me, but it was a little more special to have affirmation from my doctors.

Something was apparent: I had to accept the new me, who I became after my injuries. I wasn't just recovering anymore – I was evolving. I knew I needed to reach out to my spirit self. I needed to allow my spirit self to lead.

CHAPTER SIXTEEN

February 17, 2012

As she often did during the course of my healing, my friend Ann Marie came over to talk one afternoon. During our conversation, she remarked, "It's wonderful to see your personality starting to come back. Although I never wanted to say anything before, because I always did feel that you would recover, your healing has been even better than I thought it would be."

I was so happy to hear that – I was glad that my friends could see parts of 'me' again.

Already having shared my spiritual journey with her, I decided to show her my special piece of selenite from Polly. I explained, "I think this selenite has been helping me heal. Polly brought it with her a few times for Reiki, and, eventually, she left it with me because of the strong connection I feel with it. Well, not a connection I feel only to it, but more like it strengthens my connection with the other dimension. Somehow it extends me. It's hard to explain, but when it is in my hands, my energy heart can open up even more."

I wasn't sure how much I wanted to say about my experiences in one day. However, I still had difficulty thinking of new things to talk about, so I found myself just quietly looking around the room.

I spotted a small eagle statue that had recently been brought back for me from the Grand Canyon as a special souvenir. It was only about two and a half inches tall, but I felt something was special about it, "I just received that little eagle as a gift. It was hand carved out of alabaster. When I'm near it, I feel almost as if it can help me fly up and see the bigger picture. Like it shifts me to have a more open gaze on things. It reminds me to look at things more from my spiritual self."

"I'm not sure about eagles in particular, but you have frequently told me about seeing hawks. Not immediately after you were hit, but then when you started to see them, you really did see them a lot. Maybe they have a spiritual connection."

Ann Marie was really making me wonder, "Oh, I don't know. I didn't even know I mentioned seeing hawks with an unusual frequency."

Our conversation moved away from my spiritual experiences, but I was still thinking about hawks, even after she left. I decided to look up what they meant online. As I clicked through a few websites, I kept reading that hawks were messengers of spiritual awareness. I told myself, "WOW! I really do think they're connected to the spiritual awakening I seem to be having."

That night, I mentioned to Ron what Ann Marie had told me about seeing hawks more than she thought typical. He verified, "Yes, you've been seeing them often. Even in the car on the way to Pittsburgh to visit my family you would frequently say, 'There's a hawk! There's another!' and on and on. One time, shortly after you were back home from the hospital, there were four or five hawks in our backyard. I couldn't believe it. I've never seen so many hawks sitting so close together. They're territorial."

Ron knew about hawks and that they didn't like to be together, so he couldn't even believe how they appeared for me to see?! I was a bit awestruck. I knew for sure that they were special. They really were showing up for *me*.

I ran into my friend Cathy and talked with her for quite some time. I shared a little bit with her about how I was exploring a new path, but I was reserved with which experiences I shared and how detailed I got.

She told me, "Oh, I believe in energy. In fact, I know a lady who senses it. She even knew that something was wrong with my back/shoulder area before I told her about it."

No longer worried about opening up with Cathy and a bit curious to 'test' myself, I placed my hand over the area she had just pointed to, floating, without touching her. As I stood with my hand outstretched, I simply asked the universe for energy to help Cathy heal. I felt my crown open up and suddenly there was warmth radiating from my hand.

Before I said anything, she said, "I can feel heat."

I was a bit skeptical – I wasn't sure to believe her, but I didn't know how to respond either. I just kept quietly inviting energy in. I think she could feel my apprehension though because she reiterated, "I'm not lying, Linda. This is incredible! The area where I have been having problems really is getting warmer!"

This time, I believed her. I was amazed that she felt warmth, she felt healing, and I wasn't even touching her! I was beginning to understand another gift I had received. Polly had told me a while back that I had healing hands; we had even sent out healing energy, but no one was able to tell me that what I was doing was truly and effectively working. Cathy just did though, leaving me surprised with myself.

After our conversation, I felt rejuvenated. The more open I was, and the more I shared, the more assurance and positivity I was met with. The more I allowed, the more I could do, and the more support I felt. It was sometimes unbelievable what followed after I opened up talking about my spiritual experiences. This was certainly one of those times.

At home later, I could feel that my energy self was gaining confidence – I was glad that I had been confident enough to initiate a conversation about my spiritual path. Thinking about what transpired with Cathy, I even realized that maybe I didn't have to do things exactly like the old me would have just to prove to everyone else I was healed – they could join me on my new journey instead!

Seemingly out of nowhere, the energies that made up my panel in the other dimension were nodding their heads to agree with me. 'They' had been encouraging me to pursue my spiritual journey all along, while I was the one who asked to put it on hold in order to prove to the world and myself that I was the same 'me'. 'They' were pleased with my insight, reminding me, "You are to do much bigger, more important things on this earth than you did before."

I replied, "I need to start. But how?"

"Just trust."

I sat still to connect with the other dimension. I felt oneness – I suppose some might call it harmony. There was neither conflict nor anger, just a calm, white, light place to be. Everything was a complete oneness, and I was a part of the oneness. What an amazing feeling.

Unfortunately, I had become so busy rushing around completing tasks important to my humanness (since my brain was healing so well, I was gaining more daily responsibilities) that I wasn't taking the time to 'be' in this state as often as I needed. I said to myself, actually aloud this time, "I wish I had more time to be with my gifts."

As soon as the words came out, I knew saying that was wrong, so I corrected myself, "No, I wish I took more time to allow things to happen, develop, and unfold."

I quieted my mind to allow. I sensed some energy. Even though I knew it was not physically on this earth plane, it presented itself to me as an elderly man. He was dressed in purple – in fact, a long, hooded purple robe with wide, flowing sleeves covered all of him expect for his long, white beard, which very visibly trailed to a point. He stood silently, but then lifted his head to looks towards me. His skin was wrinkled, and even though his stature was slim and lean, there was a strength to him. Not a muscular strength, but I sensed he was a man who knew everything. He didn't have a know-it-all attitude, but rather he was someone who was very wise. He told me, "You know more than you understand that you know. It's important to keep believing in the spiritual world."

I responded, "I never knew all of this existed like it really does." Then, I noticed a cane that he held. It was beautiful with a clear, brilliant white light shining outwards in all directions. In thought words I said, "You are powerful, you have power."

He instantly corrected me "No, I serve. I only serve."

Immediately, I understood. Although referring to himself in his answer, he was telling me my role too. I acknowledged him with a sense of knowing.

CHAPTER SEVENTEEN

March 3, 2012

While attending the memorial service for my friend Lynette's father, I listened intently as various people spoke lovingly of him and his passing to heaven. The unifying theme of their kind and insightful words regarding his spiritual continuance struck a chord with me. I thought, "Gosh, they got it right. It's not death, but rather a coming home. When we leave our bodies we aren't dead, we just leave the body and go home to the great and wonderful divinity. The spirit, the oneness, the completeness."

The pastor took the pulpit last and shared his perspective: life is like a movie theatre. He shared his belief that death closes one curtain, but opens up another.

I didn't quite agree with his analogy, "No, that's not

how I see it. Both exist simultaneously – one doesn't close and another open so definitively like that. I know we can actually live in both worlds at the same time. I have felt that connected oneness. There aren't multiple curtains; sometimes we just might focus on seeing one more clearly. I can access and be in both dimensions from here. We all can. We don't have to wait for death to experience the other dimension's indescribable love and support just because we are tied to our physical bodies."

My experiences with the other dimension were finally colliding with my day-to-day life. I was using them to make sense of each other, and, as I integrated the two dimensions within myself, I found that I was able to solidify my perspective and personalize my understandings.

A few days later, I met with Polly. Still trying to help me in the ways that she could, she introduced me to something new: chanting. She shared, "Many people feel more connected to the other dimension when chanting."

She modeled it first.

When we tried it together, I stopped very quickly. I told her, "Chanting takes away from the personal experience. It takes away from my focus – I'm not able to just 'allow' because I'm too focused on chanting."

It seemed like a simple thing to realize and say, but it was important for me. Unlike others, I definitely felt less connected while chanting.

My exposure to chanting was the first time I felt like I was personalizing my gifts. I knew what worked best for me regardless of anyone else's opinions. I wasn't being imprinted. I was on my own, unique path. It was a directional experience. I had never used that term before, but I knew it was significant the second it came to me. I was no longer being flooded by experiences – I was finding my own direction.

CHAPTER EIGHTEEN

May 5, 2012

Three years after I was hit, to the date, I reflected on what a long recovery I'd had since getting hit; more so, I was saddened that I was *still* adjusting and healing in an attempt to regain me. Yes, I had come far, but I still had physical, emotional, and cognitive deficits. It was difficult to adjust to my new normal.

Occasionally, the setbacks still felt like too much weight. Sometimes, I felt lost, as if I would be going along and fall into a hole. Some holes felt deep – with those ones I didn't know what to do; I couldn't understand them. Other times, I'd feel like my head was going in circles and I wasn't even sure where to go, let alone know what to do if I ever got there. It felt like I was moving blindly. How overwhelming! It was hard to keep afloat through some circumstances. No matter what though, I kept going, or at least tried my best.

Despite the persistent challenges, I knew that I really was still moving forward. I didn't just get stuck in a hole or stay blind; eventually, I always found my way. During some moments, I could feel my brain building connections. There were times when I'd really feel like a light bulb turned on. Something would just click into place and make sense. I worked hard – I wasn't going to give up. I didn't want to have to keep dealing with setbacks anymore though.

That night, after dinner, Ron and I went outside with our binoculars to look closely at a special kind of full moon: a super moon. A few clouds were moving across the sky and the trees were reaching up as the moon continued to rise near the horizon. The moon was kind of hidden. I remarked, "The moon looks confused."

Ron questioned, "How so?"

I told him what I was thinking, "It's a bright moon. It wants to shine, and yet some of the tree branches and soft dark clouds are blocking parts of it. Not all of it, but parts. It's like me. I have this new journey I want to embark on, to break free in that light, yet I'm not fully able to yet. Something is holding me back too." I didn't tell Ron, but sometimes it just felt like I was looking for something, not a physical something, not a tangible thing, but something. I wished I knew what I was searching for; maybe that would have been easier to find because it was odd to search for something without knowing what. All the while though, I knew there was so much more.

I wanted answers. I wanted to know what was

missing or holding me back. I went to the other dimension with my energy self only to discover that there was no need to ask any questions: "It is what it is". No need to search. However, in the physical dimension, I wanted, even sometimes I felt like I needed, to know what steps to take. Things certainly got confusing in my earthly self, but my spirit self knew the other dimension's clarity.

I knew my spirit self was more important and that staying on my new path, well, my whole new journey, was key to my future. I wanted to stay connected, even build that connection. I was trying to center myself every night as a way to help me stay in touch with my energy self. Lying in bed, I told myself to shift to the side of oneness and connect to the energies from the other dimension, like the healers and the angels.

I liked the connection, the extension of myself swirling with 'Them'. When I worried about what to do in my humanness, it helped to just 'be' in their dimension with the feeling of completeness and oneness with 'The All' – such a light, airy, free feeling.

Instead of asking any more questions, I just thanked all the energy for its support in helping me heal more than the doctors first thought I would and for continuing to guide me through what seemed like my never-ending healing journey and down my spiritual path.

The more I was accepting my spiritual journey and sharing it with the world, the more I felt it was finding me. Not only were people opening up to me and encouraging me further, but I was opening up more to myself as I kept discovering things I hadn't ever known or even thought about before.

Visiting and walking through Alexandria, Virginia, Ron and I stumbled upon a small shop. I wasn't entirely sure what it held inside, but I felt called to find out. We walked up the narrow steps to the second floor. I was instantly attracted to a display shelf full of chimes. I had never used chimes before, but I knew the angels communicated in high-pitched voices, the ones that reminded me of dolphins. Chimes were high-pitched too, so I hit one.

I paused to listen before telling Ron, "How nice to call the angels."

As we listened to the note ring out, I corrected myself, "Well, actually, I'm not sure if I called them because I know the angels don't like to be called." Regardless of the exact reason, the chimes resonated with me. After trying a few out, I selected my favorite. I bought the table chime with two high-pitched bars that you strike with a small mallet.

It seemed coincidental discovering the chimes while I was searching for 'something' and looking for more information to help me find the next step on my path. Then, I remembered that everything happens for a reason – there are no coincidences. It's almost as if the world was opening up to me. I had stopped looking for the next step, and my path was unfolding in front of me in the most unexpected places. How lucky I was that these sorts of things were being dropped into my journey to help me focus and explore!

As soon as we got back from our trip, I excitedly

took my new chime out. I used the mallet to strike one of the bars. Initially, I thought, "How nice that I can call the angels!" Then, I told myself, "No, it doesn't work that way. But then...how does just one note get me with them?"

I explained my slight confusion to Ron, "I know that I can't call the angels, but then why would the chime help me reach them?"

He suggested, "Maybe the chime opens *your* channels up, not theirs."

I hadn't even thought of that! The moment he said it, I knew: the chime didn't call the angels to me, it was something that aided me to 'allow' and reach *their* vibration.

CHAPTER NINETEEN

June 17, 2012

My dad invited me to his church, the one I grew up going to for many years, for a service. Even though it was familiar, I was overwhelmed when we walked in. I remembered the majority of the long time members, and, right after the service ended, many of them who had heard about my getting hit by a car flooded me to ask how I was. They were all so kind and welcoming; I could feel their loving concern. There was one problem: no one realized how, from inside my brain, the world was different. The physical injuries had generally healed, but no one could see the brain trauma to help gauge their interactions with me. I explained in simple terms that I had two brains: a memory brain from before I was hit and an active brain that was developing. Backing out of the crowd, I elaborated that my active brain still couldn't handle too much stimulation at one time, meaning that I couldn't stay and talk.

As my dad and I were leaving in favor of a less overloading environment, the congregation reminded me how much they'd kept me in their prayers. I thanked them, "Prayers are powerful. I am a miracle. Most doctors didn't even think I would recover this well. I am grateful to have all your love and support. I appreciate it all very much."

I went back to my dad's house to visit with just him – my brain was relieved to be in a quiet atmosphere. I had already opened up to him about my experiences with the other dimension and the communications I had with those who had passed, so he took this opportunity to tell me, "It has been very difficult to lose so many relatives in one year: a brother, two brothers-in-law and a sister-in-law."

Immediately, I knew energies were present with us. The most outspoken was his brother, Uncle Connie. I hadn't channeled for a while; this was a chance for me to prove my gifts to myself again. Uncle Connie wanted me to make a strong connection to my dad for him, but I asked him for an affirmation that it was actually him communicating with me first.

Uncle Connie understood and shared something about my grandpa's health. Something in order to verify to me that I really was bridging the two dimensions. My grandpa had passed before I was born, but suddenly I saw that he had trouble walking. Looking for the confirmation in the physical dimension, I asked, "Dad, was there something wrong with one of Grandpa's legs or feet?"

"Yes, his knee."

Wow, my confidence grew. I began repeating what Uncle Connie asked me to tell my dad, and, as I spoke, I realized I was learning things about my dad's family that I never knew before. After Uncle Connie's messages, universal energy, not energy specific to anyone who had passed, began to communicate with me about my dad.

Through these thought messages, I heard that my dad wasn't taking enough time for himself. Then, there was something very important being communicated to me that I was supposed to tell him, so I did, "Dad, you need to take care of yourself. It's important to get centered and go inward. You are like a big tree with all these giving branches, but now the universe and all its energy want you to take some and wrap the trunk. You're a giver, but you need to receive some now."

"I'm used to trying to take care of so much by myself though."

I reminded him again, "Take care of yourself. Learn to receive some."

Sometimes, I secretly wondered if I would lose my abilities and gifts if I didn't focus on the spiritual me, but this showed me that I wasn't losing anything. Best of all, my dad was very supportive of me, "It's very special to have these gifts. They are meant to be used."

"I've had so many experiences and conversations that I'm finally feeling comfortable in my new skin and in accepting my 'gifts'. Sometimes I don't know if this is what I should do, but then I remember how much I feel at peace, as one, a whole when I'm with the other dimension. Like all is well, just as it should be."

"I'm happy for you, Linda."

As I was getting ready to go, I put my things back down and started to tell a story, a rather long story. All of a sudden it was as if I was being told by the unseen energy that it was time to go. I wanted to finish my story though, so I stayed and kept talking. Again, it was communicated that I needed to leave and come back another time. I wasn't quite sure why I was hearing this, but I felt the tug to go grow stronger, so I finally listened.

Driving away, I wondered why I was being told it was time to leave. Then, in my rearview mirror, I saw someone else pull into his driveway to visit. I understood that it had been my time to go so that someone else could arrive.

Mostly rhetorically, I asked the other dimension and myself, "Am I really being guided?"

I met with my friend Annette for lunch. We hadn't seen each other for some time, so she wasn't aware of everything new that was happening to me and for me. While we were in the midst of chatting for the sake of catching up, the atmosphere changed. I felt a strong energy presence. I stopped looking at Annette as I allowed my gaze to, almost automatically, shift, letting me focus more intently on the other dimension's energy.

Her dad began to communicate some very strong messages. I had gotten somewhat comfortable with this happening, so I didn't think much of just relaying his messages, "I'm getting a message from your dad so strong that I can't keep from telling you. He says he is very proud of you and the way you have lived your life. He sees so much of himself in you – you view the world in similar ways. He is also saying that he knows that you're going to be okay. He's not worried about you."

Annette didn't reply, not even a single word. Then, I got a little nervous when I refocused on her and noticed a few tears gathering in her eyes. My new brain had recently relearned that tears meant sadness. I thought, "Uh-oh! I just hurt one of my good friends!" There went my encouragement as the doubt over my gifts crept back in.

Terrified that she was about to get mad at me, I hurriedly apologized, "I'm sorry for ruining our friendly lunch."

Softly, and with a few more tears, she gave me back some of the confidence I needed, "I'm not disagreeing with anything you said. I'm not upset at all. It's the opposite. I'm in shock in such a good way. I'm in awe that you are doing this."

I was relieved to learn that her tears were not tears of sadness, but rather tears because she was emotionally moved by what I could do. I was pleased with myself that what I was able to connect with and share had positively affected her. I still had questions and apprehensions, but I was seeing that I could make a bigger impact following this new path and sharing the vastness of 'The All' and its dimension than any path I had ever planned myself.

Driving home, I reflected on all of the feelings of

doubt, uncertainty, and hesitation I had encountered on my journey from awareness to acceptance, and now while I was grappling with how to embrace everything. I asked the other dimension for a sign that I was still moving in the right direction.

I began to I reprimand myself, "Why are you testing 'Them'? You know you don't have to." I knew there wasn't negativity in the other dimension, but I didn't want them to be upset with me, especially after all of their encouragement.

Trying to decide if it was fair to ask for a sign when I already knew the answer, a hawk flew right over me, as if it was saying, "Look here I am! See my white belly! I'm a hawk! I'm here!"

Hawks had become so special to me, but I wanted to make sure it was the sign I was looking for, so I silently asked for another hawk. I wasn't looking for it, just wondering if it would fly by. A couple of minutes later, I turned my head. Sitting on a tree in the center of my field of vision was another hawk. In the span of just a few minutes, I saw not one, but two hawks. I smiled to myself and thanked 'Them' for the sign. I felt at peace.

CHAPTER TWENTY

August 11, 2012

My friend Debi was hosting a high school graduation party for her son. I wanted to go celebrate his accomplishment, enjoy some good food, and talk with some of the people who I hadn't seen in a while. I got to do all these things; however, the way the afternoon unfolded caught me off guard.

After getting my plate of food, I sat down with Debi and her sister-in-law Kim. While we were delighting in the sunny day, Kim called her sister-in-law Mary over to reintroduce us. Mary immediately changed the topic of our conversation, "Debi said that since you were hit you have started to communicate with and channel those who have passed."

Completely blindsided, I was stunned by being singled out about my gifts, "Debi, who did you tell?

How many people? I haven't been very public." I was panicking. I wasn't openly sharing my experiences yet; I was close, but I was still only comfortable confiding in some of my friends. I was working on gaining confidence and a more complete vocabulary first.

Before Debi could answer what I so desperately wanted to know, Mary eagerly asked, "I've gotten a reading before. Could you do one now?"

Flung into a spotlight I wasn't ready for, I said, "No, not today."

I had given messages to friends before, but I didn't know how to just start channeling for someone entirely new on the spot. Regardless of how prepared (or not) I felt, I was definitely feeling overwhelmed and pressured by requests for readings.

Mary prodded me, "It doesn't have to be a long one."

Everyone was so interested that I couldn't see them giving up. I was uneasy, but I took a deep breath to help clam my nerves and allow. After I made this shift, an energy presented itself. I reminded myself not to interpret anything, that even if I might not understand a message, its recipient would. I didn't have to test myself like I had been doing before.

I started to share a message from Mary's mom, "She is showing me that she's standing with a bell in her hands and a tear in her eyes."

Mary seemed moved, "My mom always referred to me as her little bell."

I didn't get any further with my message because a gentleman who was sitting a table away heard our conversation and immediately came over to share, "I can't believe what you just said! Mary's dad was just telling us before you arrived that she appears to him with a tear. I'm blown away because you couldn't have possibly known that! It's exactly what he said earlier!"

A few weeks later, Ron received a small package in the mail. When he got home from work, I asked, "What did you order?"

"I bought a couple of minerals for you. Maybe some will resonate with you like the selenite Polly gave you."

"Okay. Why don't you open it now?"

"I will, but I'd like to try something different. Why don't you sit down and close your eyes. I will place one in your hands."

Unsure if that even mattered, I agreed to try it. He put a mineral in my hands that felt hard, lumpy, and heavy. It just felt like a rock at first. Keeping my eyes shut, I sat with it for a few moments. I started to feel as if I was growing roots deep into the ground and my body was going inwards. I showed Ron by bending forward and bringing my arms inwards.

I opened my eyes and Ron informed me, "That's obsidian. People say that one connects most strongly with the lowest part of your body."

Often, I felt like I was testing myself. When people asked me to use my gifts, I would want to try, but felt apprehension about being judged if something was wrong. When he told me this though, I smiled because I connected just like others had. It was real.

Ron pulled a few more minerals out of the box. I

held them one at a time as he read the cards to himself that explained each one's energy. I wanted to see how well I could connect. Allowing the mineral to communicate with me, I told Ron what I felt from each one. What was crazy to me was that they all said something different. They each had their own unique attributes and meanings.

When I was done, he told me how well I matched the descriptions they came with, "I would rate you really well. I'm surprised because you did so much better than random chance. You knew without ever seeing them or learning about them."

Blown away by what I was able to do, I slowly responded, "Yes, I just *knew*."

"Did you know that after I handed one to you, but before you would hold it to receive messages and communicate, you would turn it around in your hands? Once you found a way to hold it, you didn't move it the rest of the time."

"Well, once I have them pointing a certain way, the way they want to face, they feel settled enough to open up to me."

"Did you notice anything different between the polished ones and the raw ones?"

Oh gosh. I sat for a moment to remember how they felt. Yes, there had been a difference! "Yes, to me the raw ones connect more deeply. They open me up with an even stronger energy. They all have energy, but the raw ones just seem like more. A more powerful intensity."

We finished going through the entire box, and, coming from a science background, Ron wanted to look at all the minerals under a black light.

First, he shined the black light through a piece of selenite that he had bought. The light went through. I was amazed seeing it, but then Ron put the black light under my special selenite from Polly – I was taken aback. The light didn't go through.

Ron said, "Yours transforms energy. It takes energy in and transforms it to give out. The other selenite just transmits it. Most selenite I've seen before just transmits it. Yours is different."

I just beamed. I knew it was special.

Putting everything away, he still looked a bit shocked by everything I had said. He wasn't just encouraging me; for the first time, I knew he truly believed everything I was experiencing with the other dimension.

Ron and I went out for lunch; instead of a restaurant, we chose to head for a market in Cleveland and try different foods while we walked around. I stumbled upon a stall selling gyros; I knew I had always enjoyed gyros before I was hit. I hadn't had one in the last couple of years, so I got in line to wait – it was a very long line. A few minutes in, I had barely moved closer. I wondered if the gyro was really going to be worth waiting for or if I should just go on to try something else, so I turned and asked the lady behind me, "Have you ever had one of these gyros before?"

"No, it's my first time here."

That wasn't much help, but I chose to wait and struck up a conversation with her to pass the time. She was a few weeks away from having her second child. Laughing, she said, "I used to think 37 was old, but I'm already 30! I can't believe how short life can be."

"I understand that well – I was lucky enough to survive being hit by a car as a pedestrian. I've heard some people say that it's a miracle I'm doing as well as I am. I'm very grateful."

We exchanged some words about the importance of being present, centered, and enjoying even the littlest things in life.

She shared, "I think a lot of my enjoyment comes because I'm doing what makes me happy. When I was a young girl, I visited my grandpa quite often in his nursing home. Each visit, I watched everyone at work and knew that I could do better than the staff was. More so, I knew the residents deserved better. Years later and my grandpa long gone, I now work in one, hoping to touch whomever I can."

"You are not only fortunate for embracing what you've felt called to do, but so are the elderly you compassionately care for." No longer hiding behind my spiritual journey, I continued, albeit a bit tentatively, "I used to love being an elementary school teacher, but I am just starting on a new path. After I was hit, I came to see how much more there is. I used to not fully understand what happens after we pass away, but I've come to know this whole other dimension."

As she nodded, I felt more and more confident to go on sharing my views, "There is energy all around us. It's here for us. Our spirit selves never die when our physical selves do. In fact, I've had some experiences communicating between the dimensions. Now that I know my path has changed and the spiritual dimension exists, I know which direction I'm supposed to go."

She said, "I believe in all those sorts of experiences because when people are ready to pass, they seem to talk to deceased relatives and angels. I believe through them."

She knew her path all along, and she believed in my new one. I walked away invigorated, knowing that I had been meant to meet her that day, feel her faith, and be reminded by her sense of knowing.

My energy heart felt light as I sat down on a bench outside to eat with Ron. I told him about the conversation I just had, "I want guidance on how to develop my relationship with the energy and my panel. I want to know 'the plan' that exists for me. I want to know the next step. I know the end point, but I'm scared about getting there."

He reminded me, "To know the path is different than following it."

Hearing him say that was a deep moment for me. "Maybe that's why I'm apprehensive. Following the path might be harder now because my brain has gotten better, and along with that has come worry, doubt, and fear. A desire to know has crept in. I have a direction to go though. I am certain of 'the plan' even though I don't know the steps. How can what 'is' be so difficult?"

"I can't tell you what to do next." Ron was right. He couldn't. However, the other dimension was always there to help me. He continued, "But I will support you in whatever step you take next."

I tried not to let the earthly me take away from

what I knew was my spiritual journey. Despite worrying, I knew I was supposed to walk through the door. In fact, it was so clear to me that I *knew* I would walk through it – it was just a matter of time and understanding. I needed to embrace my spiritual journey before I could, and I wasn't there quite yet.

A few days later, I saw the door again, still as brilliant as it was before. This time, the man in purple was standing near it. I learned his name: Kauntea. I wanted to know what I would be walking towards if I went to or even through the door, but he didn't give me an answer. I shared my concern, "The spiritual me trusts, but the earthly me has some reservations."

He encouraged me towards the door and reminded me that I didn't have to ask so many questions. I just needed to trust. I just needed to 'be'. As I allowed myself to be in the other dimension, I felt settled and content. 'The plan' for me flowed into me.

I sat with the energy for a bit. When I was done, I had a moment of clarity. Everything was part of 'the plan'. It was supposed to happen, me being hit. If it didn't happen that night, it would have happened some other time. I didn't choose it, but it was God's way of opening me up to the other dimension. It was all part of 'the plan' for me. I didn't walk any closer to the door, not yet at least, but I felt a deep knowing that all was well.

CHAPTER TWENTY-ONE

October 2, 2012

Worries about letting down one dimension or the other would often cross my mind. I shared with Ron one night during dinner, "I struggle because I was happy with my old life. I still miss parts of me even though I try not to. I like my new mission because I know it will be impactful and help other people, so I'll still be happy, but it's different. It's so different than what I'm used to and what I was happy with."

Though he understood my struggle, he didn't have much to say in response to my thinking out loud. Instead, he handed me my fortune cookie. I cracked it open: *The most we can do is our best!*

"Gosh, that's what Dr. Sahgal tells me! I need to shake off being sad about not being everything I was before and focus."

Ron agreed, "Yes, because when you start trying to do more than you are able because you think you should, you get frustrated. Then, the frustration leads to worry."

"I don't think I'll ever be at that same level, or the same person, as I was before I was hit."

"Remember what Dr. Sahgal said: you're also aging. Even if you hadn't been hit, you'd still have gone through changes."

I had what seemed like one last reservation, "I understand, and you're probably right, but I'm worried that I might lose my gifts as my mind keeps thinking faster. When my mind was slow, when it was too damaged to think outside the present moment, multitask, and worry, my experiences all started. What if I surrender to my new mission, but then it all disappears as I continue to heal?"

"But what if it doesn't?"

Polly had been coming to my house for yoga, but, since I was able to, I went to her studio for a change.

After I got settled into being in a new space, she asked, "What would you like to work on today?"

I thought about it for a brief moment and then answered, "I don't care. I don't care what we do physically. I'm here because it helps with the oneness. It helps me with my connection to 'all that is'."

"Oh, Linda, you're the only client that would say that. You might be new to yoga, but you aren't a beginner. You are advanced because you feel the unity and harmony already. Why don't we start with some yoga poses?"

As we began, my mind kept thinking and focusing on the small water fountain she had on. I couldn't shut out the bubbling. I told myself to ignore it by acknowledging it and letting it go. I tried hard, but I couldn't allow its noise to drift to the back of my mind. Eventually, I pointed towards it and asked Polly, "Could you turn that off? I'm having trouble ignoring it and being in the present. My experiences have taught me the importance of being in the present moment."

As she did, she said, "When you first started yoga, you were always in the present. You didn't think of these things. You didn't have stress. Your brain couldn't even recognize it. Welcome back to being like the rest of us!"

It sounded funny, but there was truth to it – I guess I was back to the earthly world.

Now that the fountain was off, I could better allow what 'is' to 'be'. I felt so connected to the universe. Rather, with the universe. As though there was a completeness between my body, mind, and spirit and the other dimension. A union. A beautiful union. I was so very connected to the Grand Divinity, the spirit realm.

After some of the poses, Polly said, "Move as if you're in the other dimension."

"I can't." Noticing the confused look on her face, I elaborated, "It's different movement because it is in a different dimension. Our energy intertwines with other energies. It's oneness with others. In this dimension, our physical bodies prevent an intertwining. I can't represent that sort of movement with the limitations of my physical self."

Instead of trying to move and represent the other dimension, I shared my apprehensions with fully embracing my new path, "I know the direction I am supposed to head in. It's the spiritual one. But I just don't know what *exactly* that means. I hesitate not knowing what is next."

Polly asked, "Which body part feels the apprehension?"

I shared with her, "The brain is the part that is confused. I can feel a spiritual fullness in my stomach and my energy heart. I know those parts are ready – the spiritual parts want to embrace. BUT. The big BUT. My human self wants to know the answers. I am eager to find and learn more, to take a step on my path, but my humanness is concerned with being wrong."

That concern seemed to be consuming my thoughts, but it wasn't anything that anyone could help me through. I still felt a little bit confused on my way home. I tried to remind myself not to ask anything, that I didn't need to question what I knew from the other dimension. After all, at the end of the every day, I felt more sure about those things and being with the unseen energy than anything else.

It's as if 'They' were communicating reminders to me, "No questions – this is it. Now's the time."

I said, "I'm almost ready."

Though I had gained so much reassurance from both dimensions, I still couldn't help but feel apprehension occasionally creep in throughout my daily life. The fact of the matter was I *knew* I was to be on my new spiritual path. Everything pointed to it. No matter how much I questioned it, quietly or aloud, I *knew*. 'They' encouraged me onwards and I *knew* that I was to open the door so wide, surrendering and saying, "Here I am! I'm ready. I'm here to serve. What do you want me to do for you?"

It was going to be such a life change, but I knew I was to share my experiences, the knowledge I gained, and my gifts. The strange thing was that I didn't just know I *should* open the door and walk through; I knew I was *going* to. There was no question of if, just when.

With something so clear to me, I wondered why I didn't move towards it yet, "What on earth am I doing not embracing my gifts 100%?" What a question! Something clicked. I realized that was the problem – right there in my own question, "I'm on earth, and I'm doing earth things. The things I need to do as a human. The spiritual dimension is waiting for me surrender to the grand plan and all the gifts I have gained. To be a messenger and share the vastness of the other dimension. Waiting for me to follow the path of my energy spirit self, not such an earthly one. Still my mind and just be. Surrender and allow."

I began smiling because those in the other dimension were smiling. It was as if they were saying, "Linda finally gets it."

I was learning so much more about myself. It's as if all the pieces of my recovery journey were suddenly starting to add up to something greater than I ever could have imagined. I was beginning to settle into these abilities of energy and communication.

I called my friend Ann Marie to confide, "I know which direction I am to go in, but I'm still hesitant to make the shift entirely. At the same time, I feel like I've wasted months not just jumping in fully already."

She simply responded, "Okay, but don't waste more time."

Her words felt like a smack on the head. "I will be closing a door and opening a new one. But maybe the first door won't close entirely? I'm not sure, so I'm nervous still."

She agreed, "Sure, it might be scary, but how do you know it will be?"

What an 'ah-ha' moment that if I knew it was right and I knew it was me, then why wouldn't I just go for it?

I was resolute in directing myself, "It is time."

While visiting with my friend Marianne over lunch, I debated with myself (once again…as I often seemed to) whether or not I should open up with her about how my life was changing directions. I was a little cautious at first, but I trusted her, so I began to tell her about my experiences.

Marianne listened intently as I described a few of my most impactful moments, and then she shared, "I've gone to a few spiritual people and places, including healers, before. I believe you and all of these gifts."

I was a little surprised to hear this. I had known her for so long, but never had any idea. I thought, "Now that I am opening up, the world is opening up to me too. Why are people afraid to talk about this stuff? Why didn't anyone initiate and share this amazing dimension with me before I was hit?"

"It still feels so new to me. I'm still making sense of it," I was trying to reason through it with her.

"We all go through changes." Her mom had passed nearly a year before, so, moving the conversation forward she shared, "I feel guilty about not arranging a mass around her birthday, but I wasn't able to because most of the days were already taken. My mom's church is going to do something for her very soon though. I'm really happy about it."

I kept hearing, without words of course, the word 'jewelry' being communicated to me. For a second, I was confused. Then, I realized that Marianne's mom was there; she was the one telling me. The word made no sense to me as something that would be so significant, but it was sounding like a broken record playing over Marianne's story.

As Marianne was detailing the church's arrangements, I had to interrupt and take a chance, "Hold on. I have to ask something. I can't shake off the message. I keep hearing the same word over and over. What is there about 'jewelry'?"

Thankfully, Marianne's face lit up, "Oh my gosh – just last weekend I brought home my mom's jewelry and took several pieces to have remade into new pieces for my daughter and me to wear."

"That makes your mom smile. That makes her happy."

I passed on a couple more messages that her mom wanted her to know. For some reason, I wasn't feeling quite as free as I had in the past. It felt different – not as simple. I considered that maybe I wasn't trusting as much since I had been so focused on my earthly, physical me. I worried Marianne might not be able to relate to the messages.

At the end though, Marianne told me, "What you were saying is all so true. I can't even believe you pinpointed the jewelry! You are gifted."

What affirmation! Again! I didn't have to question if I was losing anything! I needed to stop worrying about it! There was so much that I never would have known on my own, but I knew them through messages shared from the other dimension. More significant to me was that, while others had always referred to what I could do as gifts, Marianne called me gift*ed*. Me. Of all people. That sure was powerful!

I kept thinking about how much meaning our conversation had. I advised myself, "You need to rise to your new direction. Accept and allow. Rise to it!"

CHAPTER TWENTY-TWO

November 29, 2012

It was a calm, peaceful morning – not because of the external environment, but because internally I felt centered. I allowed myself to relax and my energy to leave my body, enjoying the feeling of unity with 'The All'. As I communed with the other dimension from my spirit self, I felt enveloped with so much love, serenity, and compassion.

After a while, I began to communicate with my energy panel. They were gently accepting where I was on my path and nudging me forward to the next step.

I got goose bumps, "Is this real?"

I received an answer back almost before I finished asking, "Of course it is. Just trust, allow, and follow the next step."

"But I don't know every step."

"That's okay, it's 'the plan'. Take the first step, we're here. We're supporting you. We won't let you fall. We won't drop you. Don't worry about falling into a sinking hole. Stretch out your hand and hold on. We have you. Just take the first step."

I knew it was all part of 'the plan' and it's where I wanted to go, but I still felt some worry inside. At the same time, I fully knew that all would be in order. 'They' continued, "Open your heart center and keep it open. It's you, it's all you."

I felt lucky. I appreciated sharing in and with 'The All'. The next morning, I saw two hawks sitting on a wire and then one soaring in the sky. I felt a deep connection with 'The All', along with a knowing that all was well. All was as it should be. Not to say that nothing bad was going to happen, but simply that 'it is what it is'. I was comfortable where I was in my mission. I was ready and, finally, *I was going*.

I felt a lightness in my step, some sort of inner step. I was getting my inner strength back while gaining confidence to pursue my new journey. Most importantly, I knew that 'They' were with me to support me wherever I was. I didn't need a special place or any special things to 'call' them.

I finally felt like I was out of all the holes, the sinking holes that I had been falling into along my healing journey. Though I felt ready, I wanted to make sure, so I asked, "How do I know that I really am ready?"

I got a response from my panel, "Trust – we equip you. Trust. Be at peace – be at one. It's not just 'you' and 'us', and by now you should know that 'we' and 'us' are powerful because we 'are'."

"You make is sound so easy."

"What's so hard? Difficult about it?"

"Of course, nothing."

"Well, let's go then."

"Renew takes on a whole new meaning for me now."

"As it should."

"I'm scared."

"Why? It's us."

"Yes, of course. I know in that dimension, but this one is different. I know I can do more things than I've done so far, but when will I become aware of all my abilities and actually do them?" I paused. I felt at peace, very much at peace. Complete. So I wondered (yes – I was still wondering and debating with myself) why I was apprehensive when I knew such peace.

"It's new. It's new to people, so not everyone accepts it. Your mission is to help people understand and know."

"That's a tall order. Are you sure?"

"Why do you doubt? Trust. Remember: trust and allow."

I ran into a neighbor of mine who had seen my long, successful progression. She told me about a friend of hers whose husband had recently suffered a traumatic brain injury. Her friend was trying to find ways to assist him on his healing journey and wondered if I might have any insightful suggestions.

I shared how beneficial I had found yoga and Reiki

with Polly to be, and offered to connect her friend's husband with Polly. When I talked to Polly, she happily agreed, so I arranged a time for her to visit him.

With no intention of going, Polly caught me off guard when she asked, "Why don't you come with me?"

"But, Polly, you're the one who knows how to do Reiki. I can't do it. You're the one who is trained and certified. I'm not. I was only on your receiving end."

"Yes you can. We all can. I am just a conduit."

I knew she was right, and I knew from my first-hand experience with Reiki that I wanted to help him feel such incredible healing. I also knew that I had been able to do it for myself when I allowed it. "Okay, I'll come too. You will have to take the lead though."

When we arrived at his neurorehabilitation center, we met him in his room. To begin, Polly led him through some simple movements that he could complete while seated, just like she had patiently done with me. Remembering how bad I was at mirroring Polly when I first started yoga and how demanding all of the thinking was behind each movement, I was impressed at how well he was doing, particularly his fluidity. Even so, watching him follow Polly's moves reminded me of just how far I'd come.

As they exercised, I closed my eyes and invited 'The All' in. I felt energy rays softly surround us. I relished the energy. I loved the feeling. After they finished exercising his brain, Polly had him stay in his chair and placed her hands on his head to begin Reiki and asked me to place mine on his feet.

With so much experience, Polly had agreed to take

the lead, but I could tell that I was definitely fully present in the process. As soon as she turned music on, the crown of my head opened up as an instrument for the healing energy. I could sense the energy flowing straight through me and directly into him.

At times, I felt as though my energy was inside flowing throughout his brain. It was obvious that it needed healing. There was so much confusion inside. As the healing energy coursed through his brain, I saw a rectangular shaped blockage. Something more was wrong than just fragmented neurons. Nothing could connect with or through the blockage. Nothing was able to develop. I told it that healing would take time, but there was very little reaction. I worried a bit, but trusted the healing energy to do what it needed to.

When we finished and were on our way out, I could see that he had a tender smile, as if he had communicated with the energy too.

The next morning, I called his wife to make sure she knew that Polly and I had stopped in. She thanked me, but then shared the upsetting news that he was taken to the hospital earlier that morning. I felt deflated because I knew Reiki should have helped; however, when she explained what had happened, my thoughts turned around: he had gotten an infection around the shunt in his head. I didn't know he had a shunt, but as soon as I heard about it, I knew that must have been the rectangular shape that my energy had seen.

I wished them both well and hung up the phone. I could barely believe what I had just heard. I knew there was no coincidence between that information and the blockage I had seen.

A few days later, knowing that he still needed all the healing energy he could get, I decided to try Reiki from a distance. I asked for healing energy to be directed towards him, sent out intended for him. It was as if my energy went inside his head again to help heal; it was incredible.

I was in awe of what was happening. How my energy could travel. It was incredible that I could see damage and then invite healing towards it. I knew without a doubt that Reiki wasn't just effective in my healing journey, but for others too.

My brain was healing so well; however, with that, the busy-ness of life had caught back up with me. During the day, I sometimes needed to consciously remind myself to shift my mind from racing around thinking and doing to being in the moment and allowing.

I wanted to be present for 'Them'. I wanted to listen and 'be' without my earthly presence getting in the way. I arrived at Polly's studio excited for our session and eager to take a pause from rushing around in order to focus on my energy heart. Right off the bat she noticed, "You're in a different place."

I shared, "I am, Polly. I'm ready to move forward. My mission is to serve by sharing and helping people in one dimension communicate with those in the other. It has nothing to do with me, but sharing the two dimensions, connecting people between the dimensions. Both dimensions are here. The only difference is that in this dimension we use bodies, and in the other one we only use energy. I don't know how to put the other dimension into words, the streaming whiteness and the feeling of calm oneness. I have learned that there is absolutely no need to ask anything because all 'is what it is'. We create the limitations in this dimension. The other dimension has no beginning or end, it all just 'is'."

We did a couple of different yoga poses before Polly asked me, "I know you see your spirit self and communicate with the other dimension through your energy heart, but what exactly does that phrase 'energy heart' mean to you?"

I got up. I headed over to a square of fabric hanging against the back wall that I had seen several sessions before. I pointed towards the big red heart with white wings in the middle of the piece and said, "This reminds me of my energy heart. This is what communes with the other dimension."

I returned to my mat, and Polly led us into the bridge pose, reminding me, "Feel the support beneath us."

That didn't sound quite right to me, "For me, the support isn't from under us; the support is from above. It gently pulls me upwards to support me, as though there is all this white light that streams from the other dimension, pulling me towards it."

When we finished with yoga, she asked, "Would you like if we did Reiki today?"

"No, I don't need it today."

Polly seemed insistent on some sort of resting, "Well how about at least a few minutes of meditation?"

"Why?" I asked

"It's a time to reflect and allow all to come together."

"I do that during yoga. Yoga is the union of body, mind, and spirit."

She smiled, "Not many people would say that. However, my training has taught me that it is very important to have a period of rest."

"I feel 'complete' right now without resting. I feel the rays enveloping me and us, so what more do I need?"

She had no answer.

Instead, Polly had me do a bowing pose with her to end our session, "Polly, I feel like our earthly bodies are bowing to our higher selves, our energy hearts."

She could tell too, "You really are ready to move forward."

CHAPTER TWENTY-THREE

December 7, 2012

Boarding my first airplane since being hit, I felt an electrifying excitement. Of course it was an overwhelming experience, as many 'firsts' had been, but I could hardly wait any longer as I buckled in. Unlike many people, I wasn't nervous about getting it over with – I was looking forward to taking to the skies! What is it that I was anticipating?

Well, for a while I had wondered if I would be able to feel closer to the other dimension while I was physically higher above Earth, even higher than the mountain tops I occasionally envisioned myself spinning around on top of as I connected.

This was my chance to find out!

I knew energy was all around, but as soon as we took off, my eyes glued to the window. I questioned myself, slightly disappointed, "Why can't I see anyone? Where are all the energies?"

As we climbed higher, even above the clouds, nothing changed. Flying through the sky, I tried to feel more connected. Nothing was different than when I had two feet firmly planted on the ground.

I had hoped to see the energy. If not a visual for me, maybe a way to help describe it to everyone else. I certainly didn't have the words to describe what I knew, saw, or did. I couldn't do justice sharing where I went with my words. How could anyone describe beautiful perfection? I considered, "It seems magical, but I know it isn't because it is real. It's so awesome and amazing that in some ways it seems too good to be true. But it isn't too good to be true. It *is* true."

Watching out at the skies, I was still hopeful. After all, I was higher, wasn't I?! I was still studying the view in all directions and scanning the horizon for pockets of energy. I didn't see anything. Even though I couldn't see, I felt the presence like so many times before.

I learned something very important: physical space is independent of the other dimension. I can go 'there' no matter where I am physically, and nothing can encourage it or hinder it; the other dimension just 'is'.

The plane entered some turbulence, but I closed my eyes and allowed my energy to leave. Doing so, I felt completely at ease. It was calm 'there', and there was nothing to worry about. I thought, "I am calm when I'm present with my energy self. With the other dimension. Regardless of the earthly situation, I can always 'be'."

I knew that I had much to offer with the gifts I had been generously given. I wasn't going to avoid any longer. I was just about ready to open up the big door in my life, embrace walking through it, and follow where the new path would take me. In fact, I was finding that people were more open to the idea of communication with the other dimension than I had assumed. Previously, I had figured that since others didn't speak openly about experiences like mine or initiate conversations about the energy dimension, they must have fences up around the ideas. However, I realized it was me who had been putting up the fences out of fear of what might happen when I shared. I was learning that all I had been doing was constructing fake fences – most people were actually open to, sometimes even seeking, my gifts.

Sure, I had been slowly sharing my gifts with more of the world, but I was taken aback when an acquaintance approached me and asked if I would help contact someone who had already passed away. She shared that she was having a hard time sorting some things out and would appreciate some words of advice from her late husband. I was apprehensive. This was new territory.

Tentatively, I told her, "The next few weeks are quite busy for me. Maybe we can set a time up to get together and talk next month. Would that be good?"

"I would prefer sooner, like within the next few days."

I stood there, but as I did, I knew I was there to

help. This was a chance to continue in my direction. My mindset shifted. I was ready. I walked over to two chairs and turned them to face one another. Inviting her to sit down, I asked, "Could we hold hands so that I can better connect with your energy?" I knew that doing so had helped me before, and I stupidly and naively thought that I needed all the help I could get.

She reached her hands out to hold mine, and I closed my eyes so I couldn't watch her facial expressions or reactions. I explained again, "This is really one of my first times doing a reading like this. Please be honest with me about the information I'm getting and giving."

"Of course."

It began so swiftly, "What was your husband's name?"

As soon as she spoke, he was present. I shared a little piece of information, and she expressed how much it resonated. I didn't want her to share too much with me just yet, I wanted to allow the energy, and so I asked her to remain quiet.

I saw her husband standing there very serious, almost business like. He was matter-of-fact. However, his energy was coddling her. The odd thing was that I didn't know the word coddling; I knew I'd have to look it up after the reading to find out what it meant, but it somehow came to me as I was channeling.

I shared with her what I saw and heard through the energy, "I see three candles. There are two small ones and one large center one. He is telling me that just because he is gone and his candle has been extinguished and your unity candle is dimmer, your candle is still lit and should be as strong as ever. He is saddened that you have let yours dim only because he has passed on. He wants to remind you to share the amazing light he knew you had before."

I went on to relay some more personal messages. She took everything in, and, when I was finished, she thanked me for the messages. I wasn't sure if what I had received and relayed helped her, but I hoped it had.

The next day, she phoned me to share, "I received a pillar candle from someone I didn't expect a gift from at all. Based on what you said yesterday, I just *had* to call and tell you. I can hardly believe it."

I wasn't sure what to think of it. She could hardly believe it? Well, same for me! I was blown away, but also more confident. It felt nice to share my gifts. I felt freedom showing my new, authentic self.

More importantly, what I had done by communicating between the dimensions meant something to someone. I told myself, "*Wow*, that's exactly what I am supposed to be doing. Without looking for an opportunity to serve, it found me. 'They' were right: I might not know the steps, but the goal to serve would find me." I was grateful.

I felt something reach deep into me, connect with me. I was at peace. It was a good feeling, and I smiled to myself. I knew that I would do more with my gifts. I just knew – I didn't have to question anymore.

I was settling into being my 'new' self and figuring out how I fit in. I didn't want to avoid any longer. I closed my eyes and told myself, "Feel comfortable in your new skin. It's okay. Choose to allow, to follow, to allow. Look at it with excitement, not apprehension or questions. Look at it with wonderment! Surrender."

As I thought that, I smiled again. It's as if 'They' were saying, "Yes, you're ready to not only accept, but also to embrace!"

CHAPTER TWENTY-FOUR

January 8, 2013

I was lying in bed, just enjoying relaxing and being at ease, when I felt messages coming from the universe for me. Appreciating the connection to my higher self and the calmness that was surrounding me, I closed my eyes.

I saw the door again, still with its bright, white light streaming out. I was meant to go through this life and be able to share the spiritual dimension with the earthly one. I hadn't been ready to go on before, but I smiled and thought, "It's past time."

Hmm…that didn't sound very open, so I cautioned myself, "Don't say that. That's not right. Reword it: all in divine order. It's okay to be where you are."

Regardless of the past, it was time to open the door. Now. I knew. Breaking through all my thoughts,

I felt someone from the other dimension present with me. He was telling me that he was there to help me understand. That he had so much knowledge to share with me.

It was Kauntea. He was inviting me to open the door to the whiteness. I felt as if I was supposed to put my arm out, physically, as a gesture to signify that I was opening the door and surrendering. I was ready, so I reached my arm out a bit and did.

He said, "You didn't do it convincingly. You didn't do it fully surrendering."

He was right. I knew I hadn't.

"Remember to trust," he nudged me on.

I kept my eyes closed. I was still a tiny bit leery, but he encouraged me again, "Just trust."

I stretched my arm all the way out in front of me. This time, I grabbed the handle and turned it more dramatically. As I did, light flowed out. Suddenly, there was bright, streaming whiteness all around me, enveloping me.

That was all it took!

Kauntea was proud of me for opening the door. I thanked him through my energy heart for his patience, guidance, and help. I was appreciative of his insistence in prodding me along my path. He was leaving, but I didn't panic. He communicated that his role was complete, that his job had just been to support and encourage me to embrace my new path.

I was honored to share in his knowledge of the other dimension, but, at the same time, I was sad that his job was finished. I requested, "Please don't leave me yet."

He comforted me, "I'll never totally leave. I will always be here if you need me."

Suddenly, I felt blessed with an abundance of light, beauty, and tender, loving warmth. It was absolute simplicity, pure perfection.

I wondered to myself, "Did I just walk through the door?"

I sat for a moment to take in all the incredible energy that the other dimension was offering. I changed my own thoughts, "I *did* walk through the door!"

Reflecting on my new place, I asked myself, "Now then, what's the goal?"

Then, I reminded myself, "It doesn't matter what the steps are; you don't need to know 'the plan'. It will reveal itself in time, gradually. There is no need to get wrapped up. Just 'be', commune, share, and allow the present moment! It's an unusual plan, but it's not a hard one."

As I stood just inside the door, I felt the presence of energy in the space. I really, truly had gone through it. I was meant to be in the light. I was an extension of 'The All'. I had gained the understanding that everyone and everything shares a complete oneness. We are all extensions of energy, of 'The All'.

Looking around, I noticed a few of the energies that had been guiding me, as well as some I had never known before. 'They' were glad I had surrendered and accepted and were willing to aid me further. I felt lucky because I knew I still had much to learn. I was on my way.

Walking fully into the other dimension, there was

no time. Well, at least no time as experienced in the earthly dimension.

As my energy self reconnected with my physical self, I thought about how I used to hear a phrase in church when I was growing up, "The peace that passes all understanding." Finally, I was able to comprehend it. In fact, I just experienced it. I had opened up to it – it was the true knowing that I gained through the special connectedness. I thought deeply, "I was exposed, shown and now…now, I know. I don't want to turn my back on it again. I wanted to stay connected with 'The All'."

I was centered and at peace. I'd never be the 'normal' me, the person I was before I was hit, but I no longer care. I learned there was no such thing as 'normal'. "I'm not sure who me really is, but I'm ready to be myself. No, I am myself." I reassured myself silently.

It was still a new concept, and I still didn't know all the steps, but I liked who I became. I valued my new gifts more than what I had lost. Most importantly, my spirit self was leading; I was still embracing my earthly human self, but I was choosing to live as much as possible in my energy spirit self. There was nothing to worry about. I had no concerns. I had already accepted my gifts. Finally, I embraced them too. I was to serve and share. I was to surrender, allow, trust, and be. It was a long journey to get to where I was, but now, starting from that moment: *I am.*

CHAPTER TWENTY-FIVE

Where I'm at Now...

My experiences have been much more than I ever could have imagined – in scope, in richness, in meaning, and in possibility. I never knew any of it could really happen, and I certainly wasn't looking for any of it, which might be why I struggled to embrace my spiritual journey right away and why, while it was just beginning to take shape, I didn't share it with many others. Thankfully, I only turned my back on it at first.

While considering my new and very unexpected path, I often grappled with a powerful internal dilemma: I only wanted to be a healthy 'me' again. Who I was before I was hit. Not someone new. I wanted to hurry up and heal so that I could jump back into the life I had been happy with – how did a spiritual journey fit into my personal healing goals?

Well, it didn't exactly. And that's okay. Through first-hand experiences, I now know so much better: while becoming the old 'me' again may have been my own agenda, it was not 'The Plan' for me.

Looking back, I believe that suffering a traumatic brain injury was key for me to connect with the boundless energy dimension and undertake the first steps of my spiritual journey. The severity of my trauma forced me into a detachment from the world around me, cognitively and emotionally. All I could do was focus on task completion by telling my brain what to do and then carry those steps out, piece by piece, moment by moment.

I couldn't think in terms of reflection or analysis, and I didn't even have the mental capacity to let such deficits bother or concern me. I had no attachments or opinions and zero ability to judge or worry – there was just too much in the present to concentrate on at any given moment! Free from any and all concern, I lived in a relaxed state. I now realize that when my brain was too hurt to think and too fragmented to question, it was as if I had little ego. Without being conscious of it, I was left open, more open than I'd ever been in my adult life, to accept the call for awareness that was being offered from the other dimension.

While I couldn't function fully with my brain energy, my thinking self, in the earthly plane, I was unable to be a human 'doer'. Instead, I met my spirit self, who is more like a 'being'. I now know and have embraced that I have a spirit energy self, my heart-centered self, who is an extension of the great 'I Am'. In fact, we are all extensions of 'The All'.

I now know that my views had been too narrow before, and that the other dimension is much greater than I ever thought possible. I was brought up Lutheran, but throughout my spiritual journey I slowly questioned what that meant to me. I have come to understand that my human self used to put boundaries around God, I think maybe in order to define him in words and concepts I could relate to.

Religions, as I understood them, put parameters where no parameters need to be. I have since taken away the box. The true, real God is definitely bigger than I ever thought. There is one grandness that links religions together. It is such a vastness, everywhere, that I now refer to my God as 'The All'. 'The All' is universal, all encompassing. It's the belief in the 'The All' that matters, and when you find that, it's so much more, so much bigger, and full of so much meaning. In fact, it is so much more than believing – it is knowing.

To reflect my new outlook, I even began personalizing my time at church in ways I had never considered before. For example, during service one day our pastor prayed, "We pray you, God, are present with us."

Those words no longer resonated with me, so, in my own silent prayer, I changed them, "We pray we are present with you."

That is what it's all about. Being open and present.

I now know that if I'm brave enough to start the conversation, almost everyone has a story rooted in the other dimension. Amazingly, I found that my stories, when shared first, help others put their guard down and open up too. Sometimes I hear simple beliefs, and other times I hear stories of rich experiences that have happened as recent as yesterday to having lingered in the back of someone's mind for years, yearning to come out, but only to be offered when it feels safe. Regardless, I am always grateful to be able to listen.

I now know there is nothing to be afraid of with or within the spiritual realm. I have only experienced calmness, peace, purity, and the feeling of wholeness. Being with the other dimension, I only see, feel, sense, and know good and complete oneness. I have never experienced any evil, bad, negativity, or hurt in the other dimension. There isn't even time in the other dimension – at least not time that our humanness can understand. I see the amazing communing I do in the form of energy, connecting and completing me with the other dimension, as if I'm one with 'The All'. We all are. Without question. Knowing this, I can confidently share that I am not at all afraid to die.

I now know that everything has energy. I can intertwine with it, communicate with it, send it, and receive it through my spirit self. Even minerals have energy and all speak their own stories.

Through energy, I am able to communicate with people who have physically passed on from this dimension. I am still amazed every time by how I receive such unique and personal messages to pass along – I can't understand every message, and no message is ever the same. Though I might feel confused by some phrases or find I need a dictionary after relaying specific words from the other dimension, the recipient knows, understands, and is touched very deeply. I have learned that no message is mine to interpret or judge.

I now know that there are two parts to each of us. First, there is the connected, complete, spiritual us; then, there is the earthly us. After my brain injury, I was forced to live so present in the moment that I was either in this dimension or the spiritual one. It's a bit more challenging having to integrate and balance them together.

I have found that place of alignment with myself, my true self. During my journey, I saw myself standing on a bridge. There were large green mountains behind me and in front of me a path led to a lake or a wide river. I didn't understand why, but I was supposed to stay on the bridge and enjoy the beauty, get to know the scenery. It was peaceful and serene. It was then, on that bridge, that I was finally excited about myself. Not just about my journey or my gifts, but myself, for the first time since I was hit. I now understand its meaning and significance. I am not only in tune with both dimensions, but I am also in harmony between them. Despite two different dimensions, I am here, on the bridge, to connect people.

Although I still have more questions than answers, I no longer feel the pressure of them. To this day, every time I see a hawk I know it is a message for me, reaffirming my path.

With an injured brain, I lived in the state of being. I no longer live in that state by default; however, the most important piece is that I now know it exists. After everything I've learned, how far I've grown, and how well I've healed, I can tell myself to focus on the present, let go, embrace the moment, and shift to that place of freeing my mind.

Despite setbacks and struggles, when I do this, I am able to connect with the other dimension, commune with 'The All', communicate with other energies, and even allow my energy to leave my body in order to intertwine with other energies.

My energy heart is where I connect and commune from, with an incredible sense of knowing. With a sense of oneness. Pure, whole, peaceful, and free. In fact, more free than I ever feel in this earthly dimension. It just 'is' – what is, is. It is my higher self, my spiritual self. That is my authentic, true self. To lead with my energy heart means that I approach life with an open, loving, compassionate heart. To me, that means to be open and allow.

What an amazing feeling, but what does it feel like? Before I try to explain, imagine you are blind, but suddenly you envision a brilliant rainbow. Could you describe it to me? Could you use your familiar senses to decipher and capture everything you experienced? Would the senses you use every day be capable of absorbing, understanding, interpreting, and sharing it? You may be in awe, but without sight would you ever fully understand your visual experience?

This is how I feel. Everything I say falls short. I might never fully comprehend it. It is too abstract for my humanness, yet I know there's no need for questions. With my humanness, I cannot give justice to the feeling of communing with 'The All'. As close as my five senses can describe it, it reminds me of being on top of a mountain, arms outstretched, looking above. There's a cool, gentle breeze and I'm twirling around in it. I'm free – connected, complete, free. Carefree and blissful. I fill with so much gratitude!

I now know, without a doubt, that there is this second way to not only view the world, but to experience it as well. One that our five senses can't encompass. So, where is the other dimension? It's right here with us, full of energy and purity. It truly is all around us – everything is energy. Our physical bodies limit us and it might be easy to miss if we are not open, but when we find quiet moments to pause, unplug, and allow ourselves to 'be', we connect. Not only is the other dimension always with us, it is always ready to help.

We are gifted with so much support in this dimension from the spiritual dimension. For example, I know there is power in healing energy – I have experienced it. All around is support that wants to help in so many ways, yet we don't always allow it or ask for it as often or as much as it's willing to give. But it is. It's ready to help.

Through my traumatic brain injury, my perception and perspective have both changed, affording me a new balance between functioning as a 'being' and a 'doer'. I have embraced that. I have learned without question that it's not about me or what I can do. At the end of the day, it's not my credit to take – I am merely grateful to 'The All' for opening my eyes to such incredible gifts.

It's been a long journey for me to arrive here, but I am blessed. I am where I should be – 'it is what it is'. As E.M. Forster said in my favorite quote, "We must be willing to let go of the life we have planned, so as to have the life that is waiting for us." Instead of just a knock at the door to help me see what I was missing, I guess I needed a hard knock on the head, because the life that had been waiting for me found me when I was hit.

We just need to trust and allow.

25362996R00102

Made in the USA
Columbia, SC
03 September 2018